The Methuen Drama Book of
Modern Monologues for Men

Chrys Salt is an award-winning theatre director and writer
She is Artistic Director of 'Bare Boards . . . and a passion'
Theatre Company. She directs extensively in theatre and
sound and has worked with many of the country's leading
actors. She has written several books including her popular
book for actors, *Make Acting Work*. She has edited the
companion volume to this one, *The Methuen Drama Book of
Modern Monologues for Women*, and two further collections
of monologues: *The Methuen Drama Book of Contemporary
Monologues for Men* and *for Women*. In addition she has
written theatre, radio plays and documentaries. She is a
regular tutor at the London Actors Centre.

Also available

By Chrys Salt

Making Acting Work

Classical Monologues for Women

Classical Monologues for Men

Modern Monologues for Women

Contemporary Monologues for Women

Contemporary Monologues for Men

Edited by Annika Bluhm

Audition Book for Women

Audition Book for Men

Edited by Anne Harvey

Duologues for Young Actors

Monologues for Young Actors

The Methuen Drama Book of **Modern Monologues for Men**

Edited by
CHRYS SALT

Methuen Drama

Methuen Drama
A & C Black Publishers Ltd
38 Soho Square, London W1D 3HB

10 9 8 7 6 5 4 3 2

This selection first published by Methuen Publishing Ltd in 2004 as
The Methuen Book of Modern Monologues for Men. Title changed in 2006

A CIP catalogue record for this book is available from the British Library

ISBN 9-780413-774255

Typeset by SX Composing DTP, Rayleigh, Essex
Printed and bound in Great Britain by
Cox and Wyman Ltd, Reading, Berkshire

Caution

Contents

Introduction

This selection of monologues is drawn from plays written between the second half of the nineteenth century (Wedekind, Schnitzler, Buchner, Hauptmann, Jarry) to the 1970s (Dario Fo, Ayckbourn, Gems, Duras), stopping off to visit many of the playwrights who helped to fashion modern theatre along the way. I have chosen pieces that offer challenges to your skill and imagination, and have tried to introduce as much variety as possible in terms of character, age, style and content.

My aim has been to direct you towards audition pieces that are not only *right* for you, but *right* for the audition in hand, so you can bring your unique qualities as an artist to the character you have chosen.

When you are called to audition, you will either be asked to read a chunk of text 'cold', for instance '"He's a Lithuanian pole vaulter with a penchant for beer" . . . would you mind reading it for me?' Or you will be asked to perform something from your audition repertoire. You'll certainly need a handful of pieces under your belt whether it's the usual 'one classical and one contemporary piece' for drama school entry or something prepared for a specific audition for a theatre, a fringe company, an acting class or even an agent.

In any event, it's valuable experience to research a play and perform a speech – even if it has no immediate purpose. It keeps your mind alive and your creative juices flowing.

When you are choosing your audition pieces, think carefully what suits you and what you are auditioning for. No good wheeling out your Jacobean fop for Theatre in Education (TIE) or that Berkoff monologue for an Aristophanes revival! Nor should you render your Romeo if you are fully forty-two and look like an escapee from *East Enders*. Be sensible. It's horses for courses isn't it?

When I was writing my book, *Make Acting Work*, I had an interesting chat with Jude Kelly (former Artistic Director of the West Yorkshire Playhouse) about such matters. I'll quote it again because you might like to bear what she says in mind when deciding which piece to choose.

> It's very hard to make actors understand that you are often not turning them down because they are less good than somebody else – you turn them down because they are not . . . right in some way. Actors get very upset about this and yet if you ask them what they think of such and such a production, they often say 'So and so was completely wrong for that part'. At the same time they will be arguing for a completely level playing field without any version of 'typecasting' at all . . .

Your task at audition is not only to show that you might be right for *this particular job*, but that you are an artist with talent and imagination – so even if you are not 'right' this time round you will certainly stick in my mind when I am casting a similar role again. Remember casting personnel probably don't have a file for 'good actor'. How could they keep track? But they might have one for 'tough cop', 'sexy hunk' or 'city trader'. And they'll want to keep you on file if your work has impressed.

Some parts fit like a good pair of jeans. They are comfortable. They belong to you. Something inside you keys into the character's soul. The feelings he expresses, the language he uses. His class. His agenda. His emotional equipment. It just feels 'right'. The text comes 'trippingly off the tongue'. You have the right physical equipment. These are the pieces to go for. You may be wearing them for some time, so make sure they fit.

An audition piece should be a little artefact in its own right. Sometimes (heresy oh heresy) you won't need to read the play. Taken out of context you can make it your own. I recently snaffled a piece from an old Emlyn Williams play *The Corn is Green* (set in a Welsh mining community). Out of context, with a bit of tinkering and an alternative 'back story', it worked well for an Irish actor with a line in IRA terrorists.

On most occasions, however, it's *vital* to read the play. And don't read it once, read it several times. There's an apocryphal story about the actor who goes into the radio studio to read *A Book at Bedtime*. He hadn't read the book and thinks he can wing it. It is only when he gets deep into Chapter 1 that he reads 'said Stephen with his customary lisp' . . . He hadn't done his homework; do yours.

A couple of minutes is a short space of time for you to 'strut your stuff', so here are a few tips I hope you will find helpful. Bear them in mind in conjunction with the commentaries I have written when you are doing your study.

- Find out every last thing you can about your character and his journey. Look at the writer's stage directions. They will give you valuable clues. What do other people have to say about him? What has happened to him? What drives him? What does he want? Where has he come from? Where is he now? Church? Park? Drawing room? Arctic waste? Sauna? Who is he talking to? What's their relationship? Why is he saying this now? What is the style? What's the period? What does he do for a living? What's he wearing? Suit? Doublet and hose? Trainers? Everything makes a difference. Rigour is the name of the game. Play the situation. Play the intention. The text is just the icing on the cake. If I say 'You have lovely blue eyes', am I making an observation, admiring your physical attributes or telling you I love you? How many other things could it mean? Try it using a different subtext each time. You'll see what I mean.
- Never watch yourself in the mirror or listen to yourself on tape. You'll end up trying to reproduce that magic gesture, that meaningful inflection. Unless you engage with the character afresh each time, your audition piece will become a stilted, stale affair – all form and no content.
- Practice your pieces regularly so you are not caught on the hop when the phone rings.
- Don't let nerves carry you off. Fear is the enemy and will spoil all that beautiful work you did in the bedroom. If you don't get this job, you won't lose a leg. Get your audition in perspective. Remember, if I've asked to see you, I *want* you to be good. It would be such a relief to cast this part, fill this course or take you

3

on as a client. Do me a favour and give yourself a chance! Take some time before you begin. Close your eyes for a few moments. I'm happy to wait for your good work. Breathe deeply. Engage with your character. Exclude the paraphernalia of the audition situation from your thinking. You are no longer in a cluttered office at Television Centre or facing a battalion of watchful faces. You are on the battlefield at Agincourt! Or facing the son you abandoned twenty years ago. You are not here to show how clever you are. You are not *showing*, you are *being*. You are here to bring two minutes of your character's breathing life into my room. The ground under your feet is the ground he walks. You have slipped into his skin. You wear his life. You have transformed.

- Wear something you feel comfortable in. Those biting new shoes will distract you from the job in hand. Dress appropriately. It is foolish to wear your slashed jeans for that solicitor, or those butch leathers for a poetic hero.

- Make sure I see your eyes. They really are the mirrors of the soul. If you are *thinking* it right, it will *be* right. It won't matter to me how brilliantly you can mime drowning in a vat of porridge, if your work doesn't have the ring of truth about it, I won't be interested.

So it's over to you. My commentaries should not be seen as 'giving direction' in anything but the loosest sense. But I have tried to give a few tips and point you towards a few clues buried in the language or the syntax. They are by no means intended to be definitive – how could they be? – but I hope they will help when you are doing your own researches.

The pieces are arranged in an 'age ladder' with the youngsters at the beginning, so I hope that will make it easy for you to locate an appropriate piece. Sometimes, of course, a character's age is flexible and can be adapted to work for you so I have avoided being too specific. I have left in stage directions where they seem relevant and, on the odd occasion, slightly tinkered with the text (where indicated) so it works better out of context. I hope you will find this useful.

May the creative force be with you. Good luck.

This book is dedicated to Nina Finburgh, with love and thanks.

Thanks to my students and all my friends and colleagues in the business. To Elizabeth Ingrams who as editor at Methuen was patience itself over a difficult year and to Mark Dudgeon, my current editor, for invaluable help with this collection.

Spring Awakening *by Frank Wedekind (translated by Edward Bond)*

Wedekind's notorious masterpiece is a provoking portrayal of adolescent sexual awakening. It was written in 1891 when Wedekind was only twenty-six. It was so controversial in its frank portrayal of teenage sexuality that an uncensored production was not possible until after Wedekind's death. It was banned from public performance in England until 1963 when it was performed at the English National Theatre.

The play is set in a provincial German town and deals with the damage caused by adult repression to a group of teenagers struggling to make sense of their urges in a vacuum of explanation and support. Left to their own devices they explore beatings, masturbation, homo-sexuality, and rape – opening doors to passions they don't understand and which will finally have the direst consequences.

Melchior Gabor is an academically gifted teenager who challenges the repressive mechanisms of the adult world. He is more knowledgeable about the mechanics of sex than his friends. His adolescent feelings get out of hand and he forces himself on naïve, fourteen-year-old Wendla Bergmann in a hayloft. Wendla becomes pregnant and dies as a result of an abortion forced on her by a prudish mother who can't bring herself to discuss the facts of life. As a result, Melchior, is branded a 'criminal rapist' and sent to a reformatory by his disciplinarian father who is the local judge. He is unaware of Wendla's death, vainly hoping that in time she might understand.

This is the last scene of the play. Melchior has escaped the brutal regime of the reformatory by climbing through a skylight. Breathless and miserable he climbs over a wall into a cemetery to hide. Unknown to Melchior it is the cemetery in which Wendla is buried.

In this soliloquy Melchior's loneliness, guilt and self-loathing are articulated. He envies the dead but lacks the courage to commit suicide. The bleak, atmospheric, eerily-gothic landscape of the cemetery is vividly drawn and perfectly mirrors Melchior's desolate state of mind. When he finds Wendla's grave it is planted, ironically, with evergreens. The epitaph, 'Blessed are the pure in heart', underlines the hypocritical morality of the adult world. Finding Wendla's grave deprives Melchior of all hope. His guilt is almost unbearable as he takes all the blame for her death on his young shoulders.

Bright November night.

Dry leaves rustle on bushes and trees. Torn clouds chase each other over the moon. **Melchior** *climbs over the churchyard wall.*

Melchior (*jumping down inside*) That pack won't follow me here. While they search the brothels, I'll get my breath and sort myself out . . . Jacket in shreds, pockets empty. I couldn't defend myself against a child. I'll keep moving through the woods during the day . . . I knocked a cross down – the frost's killed all the flowers anyway. Everything's bare! The kingdom of death!

This is worse than climbing out of the skylight! Like falling and falling and falling into nothing! I wasn't prepared for this! I should have stayed where I was!

Why her and not me? Why not the guilty? Providence or a riddle? I'd break stones, starve – how can I even walk upright? One crime leads to another: I'll sink in a swamp. I haven't got the strength to finish it . . . It was not wrong! It was not wrong! It was not wrong!

No one's ever walked over graves and been so full of envy. No – I wouldn't have the courage! O, if I could go mad – tonight! The new ones are over there. The wind whistles on each gravestone in a different key – listen, the voices of pain! The wreaths are rotting on the marble crosses. They fall to pieces and jog up and down on their long strings. There's a forest of scarecrows over the graves. Taller than houses. Even the devil would run away. The gold letters flash so coldly. That's a willow tree groaning. Its branches are like a giant's fingers feeling over the epitaphs. A stone angel. A tablet.

That cloud's thrown its shadow on everything. How it races and howls! Like an army rushing up to the east! And no stars. There's evergreen round this one. Evergreen? A girl.

Here rests in God
Wendla Bergmann
Born 5 May 1878
Died of anemia
27 October 1892
Blessed are the pure in heart

And I murdered her. I am her murderer. Now there's nothing. I mustn't cry here. I must go away. I must go.

Crime Passionel *by Jean-Paul Sartre (translated by Kitty Black)*

Sartre's 'political thriller' was first seen in London at the Lyric Theatre Hammersmith in 1948, transferring to the West End in August of the same year.

Set in a mythical country in post-war Central Europe, the play takes as its theme the struggle between political pragmatism and idealism, principle and passion. Hugo, a young political activist, has been ordered by a party faction to assassinate Hoederer, a 'deviationist' leader of the Communist Party who has outlived his usefulness. But when Hugo finds his wife in Hoederer's arms, it raises the question whether a political assassination or a 'crime passionnel' has been committed. After spending two years in prison for his crime, Hugo tries to explain his motives to a former comrade and to himself. But the question becomes more complex when he discovers that the Party line has changed and Hoederer is now seen as a martyr and hero. Most of the story is told in flashback.

Hugo is twenty-one. He is an idealistic intellectual from a bourgeois family who has joined the Party as a reaction to his privileged upbringing and because of his empathy with the working class struggle. He has abandoned everything to join the cause.

In this flashback he has been 'planted' by the faction as Hoederer's Secretary so he can be close to his target. He and his young wife Jessica are unpacking in the bedroom of Hoederer's villa. Jessica has found Hugo's revolver in a suitcase and he has told her of his mission. Tension mounts when Hoederer's working class bodyguards arrive with machine guns to search their room. As they hunt they finger his fine clothes and pour scorn on his Party membership. Hugo has a big bed, good clothes, reads books and speaks in cultured tones. How can he be one of them?

In this impassioned speech Hugo reacts angrily to their accusation that 'he has never been hungry' and defends his reasons for joining the party. At the heart of the speech is the question as to what price he must pay to gain their acceptance and forgiveness for his privileged past. The temperature is heightened by his need to convince them of his conviction in order to stall their search for the gun.

Hugo Just this once you're right. I don't know what it is to have an appetite. If you'd seen the tonics I took as a kid! I always left half my food behind – what a waste! So they made me open my mouth: they said, one for daddy, one for mummy, one for Aunty Anna. And they pushed the spoon down my throat. Do you know what happened? I grew. But I never got any fatter. That's when they made me drink fresh blood from the slaughter-house, because I had no colour. I've never eaten meat from that day to this. Every night my father used to say: 'The boy isn't hungry. . . .' Every night, can you imagine that? 'Eat, Hugo, eat: you'll make yourself ill.' They made me take cod-liver oil; that's the height of luxury; a drug to make you hungry, when there are people in the streets who would have sold themselves for a steak; I saw them from my windows, carrying banners: 'Give us bread'. Then I had to sit down at table. Eat, Hugo, eat. One for the night watchman, who is on strike, one for the old women who picks scraps out of the dustbin, one for the carpenter with the broken leg. I left my home. I joined the Party, and all I heard was the same thing over again: 'You've never been hungry, Hugo, why do you interfere? How can you understand? You've never been hungry.' No! I've never been hungry. Never! Never? Never! Maybe you can tell me what I must do to make you all stop reproaching me?

Rosencrantz and Guildenstern are Dead
by Tom Stoppard

This play was first performed at the Edinburgh Festival in
1966 and launched Tom Stoppard's career. It focuses on two
minor characters from Shakespeare's play *Hamlet* –
Rosencrantz and Guildenstern, Hamlet's closest friends.
The playwright constantly reminds us that we are watching
a play, not real life, in which Rosencrantz and Guildenstern
are functionaries in the service of Shakespeare's plot.

Rosencrantz is a bumbling, ridiculous but harmless,
young Elizabethan gentleman who has been summoned,
with his friend Guildenstern to the Court by Hamlet's
uncle, Claudius. Hamlet has been depressed and crazed
since his father's death and his mother's over-hasty
marriage to his uncle. The friends are prevailed upon by
Claudius to support Hamlet with their friendship and try to
make sense of his unbalanced state.

Stoppard has given personalities to these two minor
characters and created in them a comic 'double act' who
spend their time musing on and evaluating their roles in the
main action. While they wait to play their parts in Hamlet's
story, we share their existential perspectives and delibera-
tions on their roles.

At this point, a group of Players have come to the Court
to perform a theatrical entertainment written by Hamlet.
They have just gone off to learn their lines and Rosencrantz
and Guildenstern are left alone to theorise about their
uncertain future. With comic prescience, Rosencrantz
speculates about what it might be like to be dead and
whether it might be preferable to be alive in the confined
space of a coffin, even if prospects inside it are limited! He
desperately wants someone, anyone, to come on stage and
care about their destinies. He fills the time with 'stand-up'
style salvos which become more and more animated as he
tries to force other unseen characters in the wings to enter.
When they don't appear he has to recognise they have no
means of controlling the plot they are part of. He wonders
when he first learned about death. He recognises that the

knowledge must have been pretty devastating, yet the memory escapes him. He becomes almost hysterical as the speech builds and quickens to the end.

Just as he has forbidden anyone to enter and begun to feel he has wrestled back some control, the playwright chooses to bring on a grand procession of characters to underline Rosencrantz's inability to disrupt the order of predestined events.

_____

Rosencrantz Do you think of yourself as actually *dead*, lying in a box with a lid on it?

[*Guildenstern No.*

Rosencrantz Nor do I, really . . .]

It's silly to be depressed by it. I mean one thinks of it like being *alive* in a box, one keeps forgetting to take into account the fact that one is *dead* . . . which should make all the difference . . . shouldn't it? I mean, you'd never *know* you were in a box, would you? It would be just like being *asleep* in a box. Not that I'd like to sleep in a box, mind you, not without any air – you'd wake up dead, for a start and then where would you be? Apart from inside a box. That's the bit I don't like, frankly. That's why I don't think of it . . .

[*Guildenstern stirs restlessly, pulling his cloak around him.*]

Because you'd be helpless, wouldn't you? Stuffed in a box like that, I mean you'd be in there for ever. Even taking into account the fact that you're dead, it isn't a pleasant thought. *Especially* if you're dead, really . . . *ask* yourself, if I asked you straight off – I'm going to stuff you in this box now, would you rather be alive or dead? Naturally, you'd prefer to be alive. Life in a box is better than no life at all. I expect. You'd have a chance at least. You could lie there thinking – well, at least I'm not dead! In a minute someone's going to bang on the lid and tell me to come out. (*Banging the floor with his fists.*) 'Hey you, whatsyername! Come out of there!'

[*Guildenstern* (jumps up savagely) *You don't have to flag it to death!*

Pause.

Rosencrantz I wouldn't think about it, if I were you. You'd only get depressed.

(Pause.)]

Eternity is a terrible thought. I mean, where's it going to end? (*Pause, then brightly.*) Two early Christians chanced to meet in Heaven. 'Saul of Tarsus yet!' cried one. 'What are *you* doing here?!' . . . 'Tarsus-Schmarsus,' replied the other, 'I'm Paul already.'

(**Rosencrantz** *stands up restlessly and flaps his arms.*)

They don't care. We count for nothing. We could remain silent till
we're green in the face, they wouldn't come.

[*Guildenstern Blue, red.*]

Rosencrantz A Christian, a Moslem and a Jew chanced to meet in a
closed carriage . . . 'Silverstein!' cried the Jew, 'Who's your friend?' . .
. 'His name's Abdullah', replied the Moslem, 'but he's no friend of
mine since he became a convert.' (*He leaps up again, stamps his feet
and shouts into the wings.*) All right, we know you're in there! Come
out talking! (*Pause.*) We have no control. None at all. . . . (*He paces.*)
Whatever became of the moment when one first knew about death?
There must have been one, a moment, in childhood when it first
occurred to you that you don't go on for ever. It must have been
shattering – stamped into one's memory. And yet I can't remember
it. It never occurred to me at all. What does one make of that? We
must be born with an intuition of mortality. Before we know the
words for it, before we know that there are words, out we come,
bloodied and squalling with the knowledge that for all the
compasses in the world, there's only one direction, and time is its
only measure. (*He reflects, getting more desperate and rapid.*) A Hindu,
a Buddhist and a lion-tamer chanced to meet, in a circus on the
Indo-Chinese border. (*He breaks out.*) They're taking us for granted!
Well, I won't stand for it! In future, notice will be taken. (*He wheels
again to face into the wings.*) Keep out, then! I forbid anyone to enter!
(*No one comes – Breathing heavily.*) That's better. . . .

Immediately, behind a grand precession enters.

15

Entertaining Mr Sloane *by Joe Orton*

This blacker than black comedy won the London Critics 'Variety' Award for the Best Play of 1964 on the grounds of its controversial subject matter. Its themes of incest and sexual perversion caused outrage when it transferred to the West End in 1964.

It is set in a house in the middle of a rubbish dump, inhabited by Kath a sexually-needy singleton in her early forties, and her frail old 'dadda' Kemp. Kath's flashy homosexual brother Ed is an occasional visitor, although Kemp hasn't spoken to him since catching him 'committing some kind of a sexual felony in the bedroom shortly after his seventeenth birthday'. When Kath meets young Mr Sloane in the library, he reminds her of the son who was taken away from her in her teens, and she invites him to move in as a paying guest. Soon Ed has employed Sloane as a fantasy 'leather-clad' chauffeur, and sister and brother are sharing his sexual favours while Sloane is taking advantage of both of them. But when Kath becomes pregnant and 'dadda' remembers where he has seen Sloane before, the sinister truth about him begins to come out.

Mr Sloane is a 'fly', amoral, sexually ambiguous young man of twenty from the south who claims to be an orphan. He's an unnatural blonde, who is calculating, assured, psychopathic, opportunistic, plausible, handsome and cocky. He manipulates Kath and Eddie by telling them the lies they most want to hear and by using his cheeky charm and physical attraction to get what he wants.

In this scene Kemp challenges Sloane about the unsolved murder of a photographer two years earlier. Sloane is trapped into this confession, but with his usual silver-tongued alacrity comes up with yet another tissue of lies. He plays the youthful innocent, the loving son – a young man on the cusp of a happy life who falls into the hands of 'a pervert' and understandably loses his 'cool'. It's not his fault. Look how he plays on his orphaned state and Kemp's homophobia to gain sympathy. This is his stock in trade – the kind of tactic that usually works with Kath and Ed, but Kemp is not taken in and doggedly refuses to keep his

mouth shut. He becomes Sloane's second murder victim
when he is brutally kicked to death.

_____

Sloane It's like this see. One day I leave the Home. Stroll along. Sky
blue. Fresh air. They'd found me a likeable permanent situation.
Canteen facilities. Fortnight's paid holiday. Overtime? Time and a
half after midnight. A staff dance each year. What more could one
wish to devote one's life to? I certainly loved that place. The air
round Twickenham was like wine. Then one day I take a trip to the
old man's grave. Hic Jacets in profusion. Ashes to Ashes. Alas the
fleeting. The sun was declining. A few press-ups on a tomb
belonging to a family name of Cavaneagh, and I left the graveyard. I
thumbs a lift from a geyser who promises me a bed. Gives me a
bath. And a meal. Very friendly. All you could wish he was, a
photographer. He shows me one or two experimental studies. An
experience for the retina and no mistake. He wanted to photo me.
For certain interesting features I had that he wanted the exclusive
right of preserving. You know how it is. I didn't like to refuse. No
harm in it I suppose. But then I got to thinking . . . I knew a kid
once called MacBride that happened to. Oh, yes . . . so when I gets
to think of this I decide I got to do something about it. And I gets
up in the middle of the night looking for the film see. He has a lot
of expensive equipment about in his studio see. Well it appears that
he gets the wrong idea. Runs in. Gives a shout. And the long and
the short of it is I lose my head which is a thing I never ought to
have done with the worry of them photos an all. And I hits him. I
hits him.

Pause.

He must have had a weak heart. Something like that I should
imagine. Definitely should have seen his doctor before that. I wasn't
to know was I? I'm not to blame.

The Music Cure *by George Bernard Shaw*

Shaw describes this short one-act comedy as 'a piece of utter nonsense' which indeed it is! It was first performed in 1914.

Lord Reginald Fizambey is a fashionably dressed, 'namby pamby', rather pretty, young aristocrat of twenty-two who is rather incomprehensibly an Under Secretary at the War Office. He's a pathetic 'upper-class twit', who is only in Parliament because his father happens to be a Duke. He is in a state of emotional collapse after disgracing himself thoroughly in the eyes of both his Party and his family by engaging in what we might call 'insider dealing'. (Knowing the army were being put on a vegetarian diet, and British Macaroni shares would go up, he bought lots of them, but is not bright enough to understand why anyone should be upset.)

Reginald's only saving grace is his talent for music – ragtime and vamping accompaniments are his forte – but he can't even bear the sound of that in his present condition. His doctor has over-prescribed opium to make him sleep.

In this scene, as he melodramatically languishes on a sofa in his mother's hotel drawing room, hallucinating about crocodiles, a lovely lady enters. She has been sent by mother to effect 'the music cure'. She is concert pianist Strega Thundridge, a 'strong, independent, muscular woman', 'female Paderewski' who comes to 'calm his troubled breast' and educate him musically by playing the classics. Strega is something of a dominatrix. One minute she is ravishing Reginald with her playing, the next, knocking him about whenever he mentions his passion for popular music. The masochistic Reginald loves it, and realises he has fallen in love with this 'terrible, splendid, ruthless, violent woman'.

Fuelled and emboldened by valerian, a stimulant his doctor has prescribed, he offers marriage in this self-dramatising, self-effacing, overblown declaration. It will be a marriage made in heaven!

Reginald You are a wonderful woman, you know. Adored one – would you mind my taking a little valerian? I'm so excited. (*He takes some.*) A – a – ah! Now I feel that I can speak. Listen to me, goddess. I am not happy. I hate my present existence. I loathe parliament. I am not fit for public affairs. I am condemned to live at home with five coarse and brutal sisters who care for nothing but Alpine climbing, and looping the loop on aeroplanes, and going on deputations, and fighting the police. Do you know what they call me?

[*Strega* (playing softly) *What do they call you, dear?*]

They call me a Clinger. Well, I confess it. I am a Clinger. I am not fit to be thrown unprotected upon the world. I want to be shielded. I want a strong arm to lean on, a dauntless heart to be gathered to and cherished, a breadwinner on whose income I can live without the sordid horrors of having to make money for myself. I am a poor little thing, I know, Strega; but I could make a home for you. I have great taste in carpets and pictures. I can cook like anything. I can play quite nicely after dinner. Though you mightn't think it, I can be quite stern and strongminded with servants. I get on splendidly with children: they never talk over my head as grown-up people do. I have a real genius for home life. And I shouldn't at all mind being tyrannized over a little: in fact, I like it. It saves me the trouble of having to think what to do. Oh, Strega, don't you want a dear little domesticated husband who would have no concern but to please you, no thought outside our home, who would be unspotted and unsoiled by the rude cold world, who would never meddle in politics or annoy you by interfering with your profession? Is there any hope for me?

Anatol *by Arthur Schnitzler*
(translated by Frank Marcus)

Set in turn-of-the-century Vienna (1893), *Anatol* is a
sequence of one-act comedies that typify the decadence of
the era. They chronicle the conquests and entanglements of
Anatol, a shameless seducer of women he culls from all
walks of life. It focuses on seven encounters and takes place
over as many years.

Anatol is a handsome young playboy in his twenties. He
is attractive, charming, sophisticated, fashionable, witty,
disillusioned and morally bankrupt.

In this playlet called *Episode*, Anatol is chatting to his
best friend, Max, in his room. Anatol has brought a large
parcel. It contains letters, flowers, and locks of hair –
momentos which he wants to entrust to Max in order to cut
all ties with the past before he leaves town. Inside are
smaller packages, each inscribed with a verse or inscription
to remind Anatol of former 'loves'. As the friends peruse the
packages, they come across one which has the simple
inscription 'Episode' and symbolically contains nothing but
the remains of a flower.

Anatol is confiding in his friend about 'the most
beautiful thing he'd ever experienced' in his amorous
adventures. It is a memory triggered by the parcel. He
paints a highly romanticised picture: a gently tinkling
piano, a girl's tousled hair, gleaming in the coloured lamp-
light, the air 'scented with love'. He is aware of its banality,
but for Anatol the mystery of love is in the mood of the
moment. He knows it will pass and that inspection or
analysis will destroy the illusion, but for that moment,
everything conspires to invest it with pure romance.
Implicit is Anatol's knowledge that the idealised girl he is
describing was nothing more than a pretty circus performer
out for a good time. He will bring Max back to earth with
that information shortly, but in this speech he is seeking to
recapture and convey the magic of the 'episode' for his
cynical friend.

It is for you to decide the level of sexual content

Schnitzler intends to convey: 'She – was at my feet so I could not reach the pedals' – I'll leave that with you!

Anatol I was sitting in front of the piano . . . in the little room I lived in in those days. It was evening. I had known her for two hours. My green and red lamp was burning. I mention the green and red lamp because it plays a part in the story –

[*Max Well?*]

Well! I sat at the piano. She – was at my feet, so that I could not reach the pedals. Her head lay in my lap, and her disarrayed hair shone with the green and red reflection from the lamp. I improvised on the piano, but only with my left hand; my right one she had pressed to her lips.

[*Max Well?*]

You and your 'well'. There's no more to it. I'd known her for two hours and I also knew that after that evening I'd probably never see her again – that's what she'd told me – and all the time I felt that at that moment I was passionately loved. I felt enveloped in it – the air was drunk with love, scented with love . . . do you know what I mean? (**Max** *nods*.) 'you poor, poor child!'. I was clearly aware of the ephemeral nature of the experience. As I felt the warm breath from her lips on my hand I already lived the whole thing in retrospect. It was already finished. She had been one of those who had been trampled underfoot. 'Episode'. That very word occurred to me then. But I was eternal . . . and I knew that that 'poor child' would never forget this hour – with her I knew it for certain. One often feels, 'tomorrow I'll be forgotten', but this was different. For the girl who lay at my feet I was the whole world. I felt that I was surrounded by a sacred, unending love. One is aware of these things; I firmly believe that. At that moment she could think of nothing but me – only me. But for me, she was already in the past, ephemeral, an episode.

The Playboy of The Western World
by John M. Synge

This poetic comic masterpiece is about the fickle nature of celebrity, lost opportunity, the need for heroic vision and the emancipation of its main character Christy Mahon. The action takes place in a small remote shebeen (a country pub) on the untamed coast of County Mayo in Ireland.

Christy is a slight, eloquent young man from a poor farming parish who arrives in town with no real sense of identity. He is a fugitive from the law. His exhausted state on arrival and the admission that he has killed his father draws prurient interest and admiration from the locals who rally round to protect him from the law. This new-found admiration affords Christie unexpected status and he quickly accepts a job as pot boy, growing visibly 'taller' with the telling of his tale. By the time he goes to his soft new bed he has thoroughly warmed to his theme and two attractive women are vying for his attention. He begins to wonder why he hadn't killed his father earlier!

In this speech, from the beginning of Act 2, Christie is enjoying his new life in the shebeen. He is up, but not yet dressed, on a bright sunny morning and is cheerfully cleaning the best boots of Pegeen, the publican's pretty daughter who had been showing such an interest. As he polishes, he surveys the crockery on the dresser marvelling at the number of jugs and the amount of drink in the bottles. Although the shebeen is rough and untidy it is a great deal better than what Christie is used to. Even the shoe brushes seem good and thick. This is the place to be! He envisages the kind of life he will have amongst the fine folk of the parish. As he looks at himself in the mirror it seems that the treatment he has received has ennobled him and he begins to see himself in a new light. When he spots the arrival of a couple of 'stranger girls' he hurries off to tidy himself up.

In the preface to the play Synge says: 'In a good play every speech should be as fully flavoured as a nut or apple.' Take him at his word and enjoy Christy's poetic flights and lusty appetite for language.

22

Much of this play's comedy comes from the rich irony of Christy basking in the admiration resulting from his terrible crime – until his father finally turns up and proves the lie! It was considered 'anti-Irish' in its day and triggered a riot in the Dublin streets when it was first produced in 1907.

Brilliant morning light. **Christy,** *looking bright and cheerful, is cleaning a girl's boots.*

Christy (*to himself, counting jugs on dresser*) Half a hundred beyond. Ten there. A score that's above. Eighty jugs. Six cups and a broken one. Two plates. A power of glasses. Bottles, a school-master'd be hard set to count, and enough in them, I'm thinking, to drunken all the wealth and wisdom of the County Clare. (*He puts down the boot carefully.*) There's her boots now, nice and decent for her evening use, and isn't it grand brushes she has? (*He puts them down and goes by degrees to the looking-glass.*) Well, this'd be a fine place to be my whole life talking out with swearing Christians, in place of my old dogs and cat; and I stalking around, smoking my pipe and drinking my fill, and never a day's work but drawing a cork an odd time, or wiping a glass, or rinsing out a shiny tumbler for a decent man. (*He takes the looking-glass from the wall and puts it on the back of a chair; then sits down in front of it and begins washing his face.*) Didn't I know rightly I was handsome, though it was the divil's own mirror we had beyond, would twist a squint across an angel's brow; and I'll be growing fine from this day, the way I'll have a soft lovely skin on me and won't be the like of the clumsy young fellows do be ploughing all times in the earth and dung. (*He starts.*) Is she coming again? (*He looks out.*) Stranger girls. God help me, where'll I hide myself away and my long neck naked to the world? (*He looks out.*) I'd best go to the room maybe till I'm dressed again.

He gathers up his coat and the looking-glass, and runs into the inner room.

Don Juan or The Love of Geometry *by Max Frisch (translated by Michael Bullock)*

This play is Max Frisch's loose ironic take on the story of Don Juan Tenorio, the character of Spanish legend who supposedly lived in Seville in the fourteenth century and was notorious for his debauchery. It was first staged in 1953.

At the beginning of the play Don Juan is a lithe, atheistic, intellectual young man of twenty who has not yet embarked on his amorous career. It is the day of his wedding to Donna Anna, daughter of Don Gonzalo, the Commander of Seville at whose castle both families have gathered for the marriage. A masquerade is in progress and all the guests are masked. The custom is that the bride and groom will recognise each other in spite of their disguises. But Don Juan is not ready for marriage and deserts Donna Anna in the middle of the ceremony, fornicating with both her mother and his best friend's fiancée on his wedding night. Don Gonzalo vows to avenge his daughter's honour and Don Juan flees the castle, pursued by swordsmen and dogs.

In Act 3, Don Juan has evaded his pursuers and is calmly eating a partridge on the castle steps as hounds bay in the distance. He is joined by his friend Don Roderigo who tells him that Donna Anna is waiting for him by the lake, and urges him to go and console her. But Don Juan is not to be persuaded, explaining to Don Roderigo that his love has died, like the passing of a 'sultry storm'. He is almost exultant, feeling liberated, 'empty and alert and filled with the need for masculine geometry'.

This is a simple, articulately argued speech in which Don Juan rejects the complexities of 'being in love' for the 'nice' perpetual certainties of mathematics. On the one hand there is love with its 'morass of emotions'; on the other, the purity and exactitudes of geometry which transcends and outlives it. Your job is to convey Don Juan's awe at the beauty, 'the pure clear transparency' of science which he describes with compelling, almost religious fervour. This is the end of Don Juan's youth and innocence and the beginning of the slide into his debauched career.

24

I commend the play's postscript to you. It will give you excellent insights into Don Juan's character.

––––––––––––––––––

Don Juan Have you never experienced the feeling of sober amazement at a science that is correct? For example, at the nature of a circle, at the purity of a geometrical locus. I long for the pure, my friend, for the sober, the exact. I have a horror of the morass of our emotions. I have never felt ashamed of a circle or disgusted by a triangle. Do you know what a triangle is? It's as inexorable as destiny. There is only one figure that can be made up out of the given parts; and hope, the illusion of unpredictable possibilities, which so often confuses our hearts, vanishes like an hallucination before these three lines. Thus and thus only, says geometry. Thus and not in some other way! No deception and no changing mood affects the issue; there is just one figure that is described by the name triangle. Isn't that beautiful? I confess, Roderigo, that I have never yet come across anything greater than this game whose rules the moon and sun obey. What is more awe-inspiring than two lines in the sand, two parallels? Look at the most distant horizon, and it is nothing in terms of infinitude; look at the distant ocean, it is distance, granted, and look up at the Milky Way, it is space – the mind goes up in steam at the thought, it is unthinkable; but it is not infinity – nothing demonstrates that save two lines in the sand, interpreted with intelligence . . . Oh, Roderigo, I am filled with love, filled with awe, that is the only reason I mock. Beyond incense, where everything is clear and serene and transparent, revelations begin; in those regions there are no passing moods, Roderigo, as in earthly love; that which is true today is also true tomorrow, and when I am no longer breathing it will still be true without me, without you. Only the sober man has an intimation of the holy; everything else is stuff and nonsense, believe me, not worth staying in.

He stretches out his hand again.

Farewell!

The White Liars *by Peter Shaffer*

This one-act play was first produced at the Lyric Theatre, London in 1968. It is set in a fortuneteller's parlour on the pier at a run-down seaside town on the south coast. Here, fortuneteller Sophie – 'Baroness Lemberg. Palmist and Clairvoyant' – practises her 'psychic arts'. Business is not good, so it is quite an event when Tom and Frank, lead singer and manager of a pop group, The White Liars, arrive on the pier for a consultation.

Frank consults Sophie first. He tells her that Tom is fantastically superstitious and, providing her with Tom's life story, bribes her to use her 'psychic powers' to warn Tom off his girlfriend. Sophie agrees and in her consultation with Tom regurgitates everything that Frank has told her. The plan comes unstuck, however, when Tom reveals that his background is a complete fiction.

Tom is in his early twenties. He is a typical sixties hippy pop singer – a 'victim of downward social mobility' and failed family expectations. He dresses 'like a parakeet' and wears his hair very long. He has a middle class accent but can easily affect 'brummie' when required. He is not the working-class lad from a Midland's mining village Frank thinks him, but the son of a rich accountant from leafy Litchfield. Middle class was 'out' in the world of 'sixties pop so he travelled south with a brummie accent so folks would think he sang with the authentic 'voice of the people'.

In this speech he cynically gazes into Sophie's crystal ball and tries to explain how the big lie came about. He shifts easily between his 'brummie' alter ego and his middle-class self as he explains how his need for attention made him fall in with what Frank and his girlfriend Sue wanted him to be: the personification of the working-class stereotype, 'all tangled hair and natural instinct'.

Sophie's allegiance is reversed as she learns Tom's version of the truth, but in the end everyone turns out to be a liar as the truth about the characters and their pasts unravels.

Gulls and wind. An enormous silence.

Tom If I said they'd made me up, would you get it? . . . If I said,
they'd made *me* make me up. That's nearer . . . I don't know.
Sometimes I see it, just for a second, a bit of it. Then it clouds over,
just like in your ball—

He crosses slowly to the crystal ball on the table.

If only that thing really worked. If it could really show the Why.
The shape of Why.

[**Sophie** *That's what it does, mister.*

Tom *Yes, but to me.*]

He picks it up, slowly.

If I had the gift – just for five minutes to see the whole thing – her
and him and me . . . How does it work? Colours, isn't it? Red for
rage, black for death? . . . What for fake? Brown. That's good. Sullen
brown: the phoney sound I put on when I came South, mainly
because I couldn't stand my own voice. (*Accent.*) Butch brown!
colour of the Midlands! . . .

He sits at the table, holding the ball.

(*Dropping the accent.*) My grandpa used to talk like that, much to my
mother's shame: I worked it up from him. It's what first turned
them on: Frank and Sue, especially Frank. He used to sit on the end
of my bed with his pencil and notebook, just grooving on it. Bogus
journalist interviewing bogus miner! 'You're so lucky', he'd say: 'so
lucky to be born a Prole. The working class is the last repository of
instinct.' I'd just shrug in my flannel pyjamas. Shrugs are perfect.
You can imply anything with a good shrug: repository of instinct –
childhood misery – Whatever's wanted.

He sets down the ball.

What colour's that? The want? The crazy want in someone for an
image to turn him on? Yeh – and the crazy way you play to it, just

to make him feel good. Green, I bet you. Green for nausea . . .
(*Simply.*) I watched him make up my childhood. 'Where were you
born?' he'd ask me. Then right away, he'd answer himself. 'Some
Godawful little cottage in the North, I suppose: no loo, I suppose,
no electric light, I suppose.' – 'I suppose' meaning 'I want'. And me,
I'd shrug. Shrug, shrug: up goes his slum. Shrug, shrug: down comes
dad's belt: ow! Anything. I made bricks out of shrugs. Slagheaps.
Flagellant fathers and blanketless winters, and stolen crusts gnawed
in the outside lav! His eyes would pop. Hers too – Sue's: no, hers
were worse. They'd brim with tears. She was the world's champion
brimmer! She cried the first night . . . She had this flat on her own,
right near the boutique. One night I'd been over for spaghetti, and
I'd played a bit to her after. Suddenly – chord of E major still fading
into the Chelsea drizzle – she's looking down at me, and her voice is
all panty. 'You were born with that', she says. 'There's the natural
music of working people in your hands. Was it hell, up there,
finding the courage to be a musician?' And down comes her hair – a
curtain of buttermilk over my mouth. And there it is. The want. I
know it right away; the same want as his, all desperate under her
hair – 'Give it to me. An image. Give me an image. Turn me on.'
What do you do? Buttermilk hair in the churn of your mouth, what
do you do? Mouth opens – starts to speak – aching with its lies – the
ache to please. (*Accent.*) 'You *understand*,' it says, dead sincere.
'Christ, you understand! . . . I'll tell you. The only encouragement
my dad ever gave me was to throw my guitar on the fire. It wasn't
much of an instrument, of course, but it was all I could afford . . .'
(*Dropping accent.*) And blue! Blue, blue for all the tears in her sky –
dropping on me! splattering me! lashing the Swedish rug like rain
on a Bank holiday beach! I was soaked. I really was. I went to bed
with her to get dry, honest.

The Kitchen *by Arnold Wesker*

This play is 'a day in the life' of a busy restaurant kitchen. It is based on Wesker's own youthful experiences. Its theme is the relationship between people and work. Wesker presents the seething kitchen as a metaphor for a post-war world. It was first performed at the Royal Court Theatre in 1959 and received an acclaimed revival by Stephen Daldry in 1994 in the same venue.

The play focuses on the story of a doomed love affair between Peter, an excitable young German cook, and Monique, a pretty blonde waitress who is married. Jealousies and racial tensions run high, grievances are aired and tempers blaze against a backdrop of a stream of restaurant orders. If they can't work out their problems in the small confines of the kitchen, what chance is there for humanity at large? When Monique finally rejects Peter in favour of her husband, his dreams are shattered and he goes berserk, smashing the gas-lead to the ovens and bringing everyone's world to a sudden and shocking standstill.

This extract occurs during a brief interlude between lunch and supper. Soon the pandemonium will start again. It is like The League of Nations – so many nationalities working together. Everyone is hot, sticky and exhausted after preparing lunch. They are imagining a world in which they wake up to find the kitchen gone and God has given each of them a chance to dream.

Peter asks each of them in turn what their dream would be. He presses Paul for an answer. Paul is a pastry cook, a young Jew, described in the stage directions as 'suave, though not unpleasant'. The structure and length of sentences give the speech a strong Jewish cadence. He is calm under pressure, well liked and rather philosophical. He doesn't like Peter, and says so, but realises he might well be a victim of his circumstances. He can't understand Peter's violent responses, but speculates that they might all be nicer human beings if the daily treadmill of the kitchen was gone. He tells a personal story to illustrate the difficulties working folk like him have in realising simple dreams.

We learn a lot about Paul from this speech – the kind of

neighbourhood he lives in, his class, his relationship with his neighbour, his attitude to politics and his philosophy of life. He despairs of human nature, man's petty concerns and his inhumanity to his fellows. He just can't understand it. The scale of the problem is overwhelming. He just can't see how anything can ever change or any dream come true and turns the question back on Peter to answer.

Paul Listen, I'll tell you a story. I agree with Dimitri also. The world is filled with kitchens – and when it's filled with kitchens you get pigs. I'll tell you. Next door me, next door where I live is a bus driver. Comes from Hoxton; he's my age, married and got two kids. He says good morning to me; I ask him how he is, I give his children sweets. That's our relationship. Somehow he seems frightened to say too much, you know? God forbid I might ask him for something. So we make no demands on each other. Then one day the busman go on strike. He's out for five weeks. Every morning I say to him, 'Keep going mate, you'll win.' Every morning I give him words of encouragement, I say I understand his cause. I've got to get up earlier to get to work but I don't mind. We're neighbours, we're workers together, he's pleased. I give him money for the strike fund. I can see he's pleased. Then one Sunday, there's a peace march. I don't believe they do much good but I go, because in this world a man's got to show he can still say his piece. The next morning he comes up to me and he says, now listen to this, he says, 'Did you go on that peace march yesterday?' So I says yes, I did go on that peace march yesterday. So he turns round to me and he says: 'You know what? A bomb should've been dropped on the lot of them! It's a pity,' he says, 'that they had children with them, 'cos a bomb should've been dropped on the lot!' And you know what was upsetting him? The march was holding up the traffic, the buses couldn't move so fast! Now I don't want him to say I'm right, I don't want him to agree with what I did, but what makes me so sick with terror is that he didn't stop to think that this man helped me in my cause so maybe, only *maybe*, there's something in his cause,

I'll talk about it. No! The buses were held up so drop a bomb, he says, on the lot! And you should've seen the hate in his eyes, as if I'd murdered his child. Like an animal he looked. And the horror is this – that there's a wall, a big wall between me and millions of people like him. And I think – where will it end? What do you do about it? And I look around me, at the kitchen, at the factories, at the enormous bloody buildings going up with all those offices and all those people in them and I think Christ! I think. Christ, Christ, Christ! (*He moves round and round with his hand on his head.*) I agree with you, Peter – maybe one morning we should wake up and find them all gone. But then I think: I should stop making pastries? The factory workers should stop making trains and cars? The miner should leave the coal where it is? (*Pause.*) *You* give *me* an answer. You give me your dream.

Ross *by Terence Rattigan*

Ross was first produced at the Haymarket Theatre in 1960 and was later made into the film epic, *Lawrence of Arabia*. It tells the story of adventurer and scholar T.E. Lawrence, famous for his exploits as British military liaison officer to the Arab Revolt during the First World War. Despite Lawrence's efforts to promote Arab Independence at the Paris Peace Conference in 1919, Britain and France already had plans to colonise Arabia. Disillusioned, Lawrence returned to Britain and enlisted in the RAF under the assumed name of Ross. There he managed to find refuge and anonymity. But after a few months he was 'outed' in the press and discharged from the Service.

The play is set in the winter of 1922 and begins and ends at the Royal Airforce Depot near London where Lawrence had enlisted. Ross has appeared before a disciplinary tribunal for failing to report back to base after a motorcycle accident and ends up being charged with gross insubordination. He can't resist telling the tribunal that he was on the way home from supper with 'Lord and Lady Astor, Mr and Mrs Bernard Shaw and the Archbishop of Canterbury.' The story of his 'insubordination' soon gets round the depot, endearing him to some of his colleagues in 'B Flight'. But sharp-witted Aircraftman Dickinson, Lawrence's escort at the tribunal, already has suspicions about Ross's identity. Lawrence's indiscreet admission confirms them.

Aircraftman Dickinson is in his twenties. He is urbane, arrogant, public school educated, ambitious, unprincipled and meticulous in his adherence to service discipline. He had a wartime commission in the army, saw action at the front and after being demobbed, got a job selling cars. Preferring service-life he joined the RAF but was turned down for a commission. He joined anyway, determined to work his way through the ranks.

Dickinson has already checked out the truth about Lawrence's supper engagement and is taunting him with his knowledge. He is rather pleased with himself, believing he has the upper hand. His tone is relaxed, patronising and not a little threatening. He dislikes Lawrence, is jealous of his natural leadership qualities and enjoys pointing out Lawrence's hubris. Look, for example, at the language he uses to describe it – the sarcastic self-deprecatory reference to himself as 'humble captain' and the demeaning over familiar use of 'old boy'. He thinks Lawrence must be involved in some clandestine activity at the depot, so will pay for his silence rather than allow his cover to be blown. Dickinson wants 'a hundred pounds to keep his trap shut' but he has completely misread the situation and the man.

I have added a few speeches that lead into this one, to clarify the context for you.

———————

[**Dickinson** *Why do you sit like that?*

Lawrence *I always do.*

Dickinson *It's the way the Arabs sit, isn't it?*

Lawrence *I don't know.*

Dickinson (*squatting beside him*) *But you should know – shouldn't you – after all that liaison work you did in the Middle East in the last war?*

Lawrence *I'm sorry. I wasn't paying attention. Yes, it's the way the Arabs sit.*

Dickinson *Damned uncomfortable it looks. Why are you shivering?*

Lawrence *I've got a touch of malaria.*

Dickinson *Middle East, I suppose? You're shaking quite badly. You'd better see the MO.*

Lawrence *No. I'll have a temperature tonight and tomorrow it'll be gone.*

Dickinson *Yes, but you shouldn't take risks, old chap. After all, we don't want to lose you, do we?*

Lawrence *I doubt if B Flight would notice.*

Dickinson *I wasn't talking about B Flight. I was talking about the nation.*]

Lawrence *puts down the notebook at last, and stares steadily at* **Dickinson**.

Aren't you going to say what on earth do you mean? Aren't you going to try and act it out just a little longer?

Pause. **Lawrence**, *staring at him steadily, says nothing.*

I agree, old boy. Useless. At the same time I notice you're not falling into the trap of saying 'How on earth did you find out?' and so confirming what might, after all, be only a wild guess. Secret Agent training, no doubt. Well, it isn't a guess. It *was* until this morning, I grant. As a matter of fact I did see you once, in Paris, in 1919 – Peace Conference time – I was just a humble captain, walking down a street and suddenly I was shoved back against some railings by some brawny gendarmes and practically squashed to death by an hysterical crowd because *you* were leaving your hotel. I couldn't see you well, but *I* remember you walking shyly – oh so shyly – between two policemen – to your car, head well down under that Arab headdress and then – at the car – turning to talk to someone so that the crowd grew even more hysterical, and then, when you were in the car, modestly pulling down the blind. Still, I wouldn't necessarily have recognized you, old boy, from that – nor even from the lecture I went to at the Albert Hall which was supposed to be about the Palestine Campaign, but which had your picture on every other slide – very carefully posed, old boy, I hope you don't mind my saying.

He offers a cigarette to **Lawrence**, *who shakes his head silently.* **Dickinson** *lights one for himself.*

Still think I'm guessing? Look, old chap, it isn't awfully hard – even for a humble airman like me – to find out the telephone number of Cliveden House, to ring up and ask if there'd been a raincoat left behind last night by Colonel Lawrence. 'Colonel Lawrence, sir?' Well-trained, this footman evidently. 'Yes, for heaven's sake – Colonel Lawrence – my dear man – Oh, very well, then, Aircraftman Ross, if you like.' Slight pause. Then 'No, sir. The Colonel left nothing behind last night. In fact I distinctly remember when he left that he had his raincoat strapped on to the back of his motor bicycle.' (*Pause.*) Your hand really *is* shaking badly. I honestly think you'd better see the MO, old boy. After all, you can't do punishment drill with malaria.

The Glass Menagerie
by Tennessee Williams

This lyrical 'memory' play premiered in 1945 and established Tennessee Williams as a major playwright. It is considered a masterwork of modern theatre.

The drama centres on the dysfunctional Wingfield family and their struggle for survival during the American Depression. Ageing southern belle Amanda, who clings desperately to another time and place, shares a cramped apartment in downtown St. Louis with her daydreaming son Tom and handicapped daughter Laura. All of them in their different ways long for escape. The children's father abandoned the family and Tom, a poet who works in a warehouse, now supports them. It is a job he loathes. Tom is torn between his familial duties and dreams of adventure, travel and becoming a writer, tensions that he sublimates through nightly trips to the cinema.

This is the opening speech of the play, all of which takes place in Tom's memory. As he tells us, he is 'the narrator of the play, but also a character in it'. He is describing precisely the nature of the play and the characters we are about to see, addressing the audience directly.

Tom is a young man with a heart full of hopes – a misunderstood outsider trapped in a world he didn't want to be in by the demands of an overbearing mother and the needs of a fragile sister. In Tennessee Williams' words, 'his nature is not remorseless but to escape from a trap he has to act without pity'. He is now a merchant seaman and a poet who has followed in the footsteps of the father who left them sixteen years earlier. His dreams have been realised and he is taking us back down memory lane to retrace the steps that brought him to this place. He comments on his world, its context, the characters in it and the symbolism he employs with a poet's eye. Yet underpinning everything is a haunting sense of something lost. Guilt is like a taste on the tongue. Although he has abandoned this world in a physical sense, what he left behind will always dog his journey.

Consider why he might be telling us all this. Is it simply

to tell his story or to validate his own selfish actions? Read Tom's last speech in the play and you will catch the flavour of this one more readily.

Tom Yes, I have tricks in my pocket, I have things up my sleeve. But I am the opposite of a stage magician. He gives you illusion that has the appearance of truth. I give you truth in the pleasant disguise of illusion.

To begin with, I turn back time. I reverse it to that quaint period, the thirties, when the huge middle class of America was matriculating in a school for the blind. Their eyes had failed them, or they had failed their eyes, and so they were having their fingers pressed forcibly down on the fiery Braille alphabet of a dissolving economy.

In Spain there was revolution. Here there was only shouting and confusion. In Spain there was Guernica. Here there were disturbances of labor, sometimes pretty violent, in otherwise peaceful cities such as Chicago, Cleveland, Saint Louis . . . This is the social background of the play.

Music begins to play.

The play is memory. Being a memory play, it is dimly lighted, it is sentimental, it is not realistic. In memory everything seems to happen to music. That explains the fiddle in the wings.

I am the narrator of the play, and also a character in it. The other characters are my mother, Amanda, my sister, Laura, and a gentleman caller who appears in the final scenes. He is the most realistic character in the play, being an emissary from a world of reality that we were somehow set apart from. But since I have a poet's weakness for symbols, I am using this character also as a symbol; he is the long-delayed but always expected something that we live for.

40

There is a fifth character in the play who doesn't appear except in this larger-than-life-size photograph over the mantel. This is our father who left us a long time ago. He was a telephone man who fell in love with long distances; he gave up his job with the telephone company and skipped the light fantastic out of town . . .

The last we heard of him was a picture postcard from Mazatlan, on the Pacific coast of Mexico, containing a message of two words: 'Hello – Goodbye!' and no address. I think the rest of the play will explain itself . . . .

Woyzeck *by Georg Büchner*
(translated by John Mackendrick)

Büchner left a fragmentary and incomplete text of the last
of his three stage plays, *Woyzeck,* when he died of typhus in
1837 aged twenty-three. It was not staged until over six
decades later and it was over a century before it received an
English translation. Nevertheless it is considered to be the
first truly 'modern' play and a forerunner of both
naturalistic and expressionistic theatre.

It tells the story of Woyzeck, a working-class enlisted
soldier who is driven mad by social deprivation, de-
humanising military discipline and the relentless abuse of
his superiors. Goaded by voices and hallucinations he slits
the throat of his slatternly common law wife, Marie, who
has been unfaithful with a Drum Major, and then drowns
himself.

Büchner attempts to make sense of Woyzeck's crime and
descent into madness by homing in on twenty-five
dislocated episodes from his life. In each scene the world
seems to torment and conspire against him, as Woyzeck is
betrayed by a capitalist society and systematically stripped
of his humanity.

Scene twenty-three takes place in the woods by a pond
where the murder has happened. Woyzeck has been
confronted and harangued by suspicious neighbours about
the blood on his hands. Fearful of discovery, he runs off and
returns to the scene of his crime. He finds Marie's body but
seems incapable of understanding what he has done. He
appears to have lost his mind completely, holding and
talking to her like a child. Her slashed neck becomes a
necklace given to her by an admirer, the blood a result of
fighting. He tries to tidy her dishevelled hair so she looks
her best, before dragging her body into the water to wash
away both their sins.

The play is thought to be based on a real-life murder
committed by a barber named Woyzeck in the 1820s.

The woods. **Marie**'s *body where it fell.* **Woyzeck** *comes through the shadows.*

Woyzeck Getting closer. Closer

This is a strange place. Weird. – What's that?

Something moving. – Shh. Just there.

— Marie?

He moves and stumbles on to the body. It shows bloody in the light.

Aah!

Marie.

— So still. – Everything so still.

He kneels on one knee by the body. Pulls the trunk up on to him resting her back on his knee, holding her like a child.

Why're you so pale, Marie?

What's that red thing round your neck? Is it a necklace?

Who gave you a necklace to commit sins with him?

Oh, you were black with them, black.

Have I made you white again?

Why's your hair so wild, Marie? – Didn't you comb it today?

So, I'll tidy it for you. You have to look your best, there'll be people to meet.

What're all these marks? Look. Here, here. Like bloodstains.

How did you get them? Have you been fighting, Marie?

Stars to lift the body.

You have to get up now, then I can wash you.

It's not far. Up.

44

Stands upright with the body held in front of him.

There's water here, to wash you. To wash everything away, then you'll be clean. – Come to the water.

Drags her down to the pool side.

D'you see the moon, Marie? There's even blood on the moon.

But you'll be clean.

Take a step. Then another.

And another.

Another.

— Water, Marie. All the water in the world to wash you. Water —

They disappear into the pool. Silence.

The National Health (*Speech 1*)
by Peter Nichols

Peter Nichols' hit black comedy is set in a male ward in a crumbling National Health hospital in the 1960s. It is a satirical and sometimes tragic examination of conditions in the National Health Service at that time, focusing on six male inmates on various journeys towards recovery or death. It received its first production at the National Theatre in 1969.

Barnet is a young hospital orderly responsible for washing, dressing, lifting, and walking the patients, besides anything else that needs doing round the ward. I have included two of his speeches here. Both are great fun, addressed directly to the audience, and take place out of the main action which always works well.

Barnet is a chirpy, 'camp', engaging and colourful character straight out of a *Carry On* film. In both the National production and the subsequent film the role was created by *Carry On* actor Jim Dale. Barnet's stock in trade is the saucy innuendo and naughty aside. He cheers and entertains the ward (and the audience) with his graphic language and black humour, all couched in his beautifully timed patter. In another life he could have been a stand up comic. He cares for the patients, takes pride in his work, is good at his job and is very central to life on the ward.

His other function is to comment on the action. He makes observations, explaining procedures or simply sharing little asides with the audience. Approaching them with endearing intimacy, he lures them into his world, embracing them and enjoying their participation.

One of Barnet's many responsibilities is to clean up and prepare corpses for public view. He is about to work the miracle on Rees, an old boy who has just died. He gets an almost womanly thrill out of his meticulously laid out instruments, bantering with individual members of the audience ('Yes, missis . . .' – very Kenneth Williams), proudly exhibiting the instruments of his craft and describing with witty and iconoclastic relish the grisly necessity of plugging the corpse's orifices.

Barnet [(to Spotman) *You'll get your cards tomorrow.* (then to **Audience**) *No, but seriously.*] Sometimes the first call you get when you come on duty is: bring your trolley. I like to see my apparatus laid out like a tea-service, every instrument in its place. With a nice white cloth. It really brings me on to see that . . . you know? (*Gooses himself.*) Here! (*Slaps his own hand.*) Lady there knows what I mean. No, but look – (*whips off cloth, shows articles as he names*): Wash bowl, sponges, nail brush and file. Safety razor, scissors, tweezers. Cotton-wool, carbolic soap. Shroud.

Covers it again. **Staff** *has gone off.*

Covered with a sheet, 'case one of the other patients catching a butcher's thinks it's all for him. So anyway I get the call. Ward such-and-such, bed so-and-so. Screens already up, of course.

Nurses *have been putting screens round* **Rees's** *bed.*

First you strip the patient down, then you wash him spotless with carbolic. Cut the nails – they can scag the shroud. Shave the face and trim the head. Comb what's left. Well, relatives don't want to find themselves mourning a scruff. Now the cotton-wool. Can anyone tell me what I do with that? (*Reacts to same* **Woman** *in audience.*) You're right, madam, absolutely right. Been making that answer all your life and for the first time it's accurate, not just vulgar. Yes. We have to close the apertures, the points that might evacuate bodily fluids. Miss one out, they'll raise Cain in the mortuary. Lug-holes, cake-holes, nose-holes, any other holes, all right madam thank you very much indeed! (*More ogling the* **Woman**.) What next? Tie the how's-your-father with a reef-knot. Seriously. You reckon I'm in jest? You'll all be getting it sooner or later. Yes, missis, even you, in a manner of speaking. (*Moves and looks at screens.*)

Thank you very much, miss.

*An **Oriental Nurse** comes on, takes the trolley. **Barnet** pats her rump as she passes. She gives shocked magician's-assistant smile to **Audience**, goes off.*

Barnet *has gone to other side to meet, rolling on, another vehicle, like a stretcher but with a hooped hood.*

(*Sings.*) Roll along, covered wagon, roll along. No, listen! I must say this in all seriousness. Everything within reason is done to spare you the sight of an actual cadaver. This hooped cover, the screens.

Nurses *cover the exit from **Rees**'s bed with screens.*

A screened passageway is put up all the way to the door, as with royalty going to the toilet. You've heard about that, haven't you? If the monarch is unusually tall, attentive observers can spot the coronet bobbing up and down all the way to the velvet convenience.

*Pushes hooped trolley upstage. **Nurse** catches it and takes it behind screens.*

No, I don't wish to give the wrong impression. I'm sure I speak for my colleagues throughout the business when I say that we show every conceivable respect the deceased is due. We may hate the sight of them when they're living but once they've passed on, they get the full going-over. And I don't know about you, but I find that thought consoling. Whatever kind of shit is thrown at us during our long and dusty travail, we can at least feel confident that, after our final innings, as we make our way to that great pavilion in the sky – no, come on – we shall be a credit to Britain's barbers, the National Health and – last but by no means least – our mothers. Thank you very much indeed.

The National Health (*Speech 2*)
by Peter Nichols

Another of Barnet's duties is to shave a patient's 'nether regions' before their operations. Again he proudly displays his equipment, neatly laid out for audience approval.

Here he is preparing Ash, an ex-teacher turned clerk who 'never lost his interest in young boys', for an operation on a perforated ulcer. He chats to the recumbent Ash, so as to take his mind off an unpleasant procedure, and engages the audience in the activity as he wields his cut-throat, sharing anecdotes about his predecessor, Vernon, who took rather too much pleasure in his work. Are these homosexual anecdotes ones in which Ash might also be interested? Barnet addresses him as a bit of a kindred spirit – teaching being 'a socially acceptable sublimation' for homosexual urges in his book. What kind of relationship did Barnet have with the unfortunate Vernon? Are these temptations ones he wrestles with himself?

Don't get too hung up on miming the actions. The minimum will suffice.

Barnet has a couple of other speeches of a similar ilk which you might be keen to look at when you read this play.

_____

Barnet. [(to **Spotman**) *Better.*] (*Looks at trolley, whips off cloth.*) A woman's work is never done. Look here – shaving brush, some lathery soap, a mug of hot water, an old strop and a cut-throat.

Nurses *are seen in the light spilt from the spot. They come on and prepare* **Ash** *for operation, putting on a white smock, etc.*

Not that it's going to get near many *throats* today. Quite the reverse – all right, madam, we know you're always the first to savvy smut. Nothing to be proud of. They'll laugh at anything, some people. This has got to be done. Not to make them beautiful, no, it's sanitation.

Ash *wheeled forward in bed so that he is between* **Barnet** *and* **Audience.** *As one of the* **Nurses** *passes* **Barnet**, *he gooses her with the shaving brush. She makes shocked face.*

Thank you ladies. Now let's see – (*Lifts bedding to expose* **Ash** *to him.*) Lie on your right side. Now relax. I know it's difficult, you naturally tend to recoil from anything nasty – unlike some I could touch with a very short stick —

Glances at **Woman** *in* **Audience.** **Ash** *makes indistinct comments and sounds during this monologue.* **Barnet** *lathers brush and then* **Ash***'s stomach.*

Which is why I try to keep talking, take their minds off it. If it's a Jew, I might ask for the loan of a fiver and that so frightens him I get on better. Now the man who used to do this job – well, it wasn't so much a *job* to him, it was a labour of love! We used to issue tin trousers whenever he was on duty. No – hospital barber, very good at short-back-and-sides, but they took him off pre-operatives. They had to, after a patient complained he'd had his privates shaved when he was only going to have his tonsils out. (*Starts to strop the razor.*) Personally I thought it was a shame. I sympathize with the customer, yes, and Vernon never learnt to hide the pleasure it gave him. But. It's not a vocation many are drawn to and most of the healing arts are bent if you want my frank opinion. (*Begins shaving.*) Now don't flinch or you'll do yourself a mischief. I've no idea what your convictions are about this highly controversial issue. You were a teacher, that's the same country. A socially acceptable sublimation. Take this case described in a medical journal I bought one afternoon in Soho. This poor berk said to his psychiatrist, he said, Doctor, Doctor, I've got a problem; I find I only fancy thirteen-year-old boys. So the Doctor said, Well, everyone to his taste, it's tricky but not insuperable. And the patient said, yes but only thirteen-year-old boys with a wet chest cough. And, d'you know, it was enough for him to *hear* them cough. Now I'm going to ask you to hold your own, if you'd be so kind. Down out of the way, you've got the idea.

Goes to shave, reacts to **Audience** *with arch disapproval. Then shaves.*

Anyway, d'you know how they fixed him up? He's a voluntary health visitor to the children's ward of a large London chest hospital! Welfare work combined with harmless pleasure, the secret of a happy life. But because poor old Vernon overstepped the mark, he's probably up the West End every night exposing himself to all and sundry . . . I've no idea what your views are but I feel a useful person should not be made a scapegoat because of one misdemeanour . . . did I tickle? I sometimes think I should charge. Never mind. All over now and very comical you look, if you'll pardon my saying so.

The Life of Galileo *by Bertolt Brecht (translated by Desmond I. Vesey)*

An early version of this play was first produced in Zurich in 1943. It poses questions at the interface between science and religion and examines the scientist's responsibility to the truth when personal safety is at stake.

Fourteen scenes take us through the life and work of the great seventeenth-century Italian astronomer Galileo, focusing on his conflict with the Catholic Church over his discovery that the earth orbits the sun. The Church, seeing his findings as a challenge to Papal power, threatens him with the Holy Inquisition. Galileo recants, not prepared to sacrifice his life for his ideas.

This pivotal speech comes in Scene 8, titled A Conversation. The Little Monk is telling Galileo the verdict of the Papal astronomer on his work. He is troubled. Not only is he a man of God, he is also a mathematician and astrologer. A scientist by training and inclination, he is torn between the decree that Galileo's findings are heretical and the evidence of his own astrological research. After nights of heart searching he concludes it is dangerous for mankind to dabble in too much science and decides to give up astronomy. Here, he explains to Galileo why he has reached his decision. As he evokes his impoverished family's life of hardship and struggle, he tries to reassure Galileo that there is wisdom and compassion in the Church's conclusions – that the threat of torture is not the only reason for accepting them.

The Little Monk comes from lowly peasant stock and is defending the Church's paternalism not just from religious conviction but from life experience. He is expressing real concerns about the impact Galileo's theories might have on his parent's faith, sense of security and hopes for salvation. He makes a cogent and compassionately argued case on their behalf for the maintenance of the status quo. In the end The Little Monk is converted to Galileo's view that the findings of science must not be suppressed, but the challenge of the piece is to communicate just how passionately The Little Monk believes in everything he must finally reject.

In the final scene, Gallileo's *Discorsi* is smuggled out of
Italy in a chest, surviving in any event!

The Little Monk I understand your bitterness. You are thinking of
certain exceptional powers which the Church can command.

[*Galileo Just say instruments of torture.*]

The Little Monk But I would mention other reasons. Let me speak
for a moment of myself. I grew up as a son of peasants in the
Campagna. They were simple people. They knew all about olive-
trees, but very little else. While observing the phases of Venus, I can
see my parents, sitting by the hearth with my sister, eating their
cheese. I see above them the beams blackened by centuries of
smoke, and I see clearly, their old, work-worn hands and the little
spoons they hold. They are not rich, but even in their misfortune
there lies concealed a certain invisible order of things. There are
those various rounds of duties, from scrubbing the floor, through
the seasons in the olive grove, to the payment of taxes. There is
even regularity in the disasters that befall them. My father's back
becomes bent, not suddenly, but more and more each spring among
the olive-trees, just as the childbearings which have made my
mother less and less a woman have followed one another at regular
intervals. But they call up the strength to sweat up the stony paths
with their baskets, to bear children, yes, even to eat, from the
feeling of continuity and necessity which is given them by the sight
of the soil, of the trees springing with new green foliage every year,
of the little church, and by listening every Sunday to the Bible texts.
They have been assured that the eye of God rests upon them;
searchingly, yes, almost anxiously – that the whole universe has
been built up round them in order that they, the actors, can play
their greater or lesser parts. What would my people say if they
learned from me that they were really on a little bit of rock that
ceaselessly revolves in empty space round another star, one among
very many, a comparatively unimportant one? Why is such

patience, such acceptance of their misery, either necessary or good today? Why is there still virtue in Holy Writ, which explains everything and has established the necessity of toil, endurance, hunger, resignation, and which now is found to be full of errors? No, I see their eyes grow frightened! I see them dropping their spoons on the hearth-stone, I see how they feel cheated and betrayed. So there is no eye resting upon us, they say. We must look after ourselves, untaught, old and worn out as we are? No one has provided a part for us on this earthly, miserable, tiny star which is not independent and round which nothing revolves? There is no meaning in our misery, hunger is simply not-having-eaten, and not a test of strength; exertion is just stooping and tugging – with nothing to show. So do you understand that in that decree of the Holy Congregation I perceive true maternal compassion, great goodness of soul?

The Devils *by John Whiting*

The action of this play takes place mainly in the French town of Loudun, and briefly in Paris, between 1623 and 1634. It is based on Aldous Huxley's book, *The Devils of Loudon*, which might be useful for your research. First performed by the Royal Shakespeare Company in 1961, it was subsequently adapted as a controversial film, directed by Ken Russell, that you might also find useful to watch.

Its themes are sexual repression, religious mania, bigotry and political intrigue during the witch-hunts of seventeenth-century France, and the search of the central character, Urbain Grandier, for a meaningful relationship with God.

Urbain Grandier is the popular, charismatic young vicar of St Peter's Church in Loudun. He is a scholar and a poet, a deeply religious man but with wayward, libertarian views. His refusal to accept the order that self-government of provincial towns like Loudun must be brought to an end puts him on a collision course with the State and Church hierarchy. This leads to fabricated accusations of witchcraft for which he is tried, tortured and finally burned at the stake.

In this speech Grandier has just come back to town on a brilliant morning after officiating at the bedside of a dying man. He is carrying flowers but has no idea where he picked them. He talks to his friend the town Sewerman who comments that he seems 'drunk with mystery'. This is a simple and poetic speech in which Grandier describes a religious experience through which he has come to understand the nature of God. In short evocative sentences he describes the scene in the old man's house. His love of humanity, with all its faults, vulgarity and foibles, his awe at the beauty of the world and his realisation of God's presence in all things, shine through the text like jewels. Everything is given an equal weight as a constituent of God's magnificence, which he has finally come to know.

Grandier I've been out of the town. An old man was dying. I sat with him for two nights and a day. I was seeing death for the hundredth time. It was an obscene struggle. It always is. Once again a senile, foolish, and sinful old man had left it rather late to come to terms. He held my hand so tightly that I could not move. His grimy face stared up at me in blank surprise at what was happening to him. So I sat there in the rancid smell of the kitchen, while in the darkness the family argued in whispers, between weeping, about how much money there would be under the bed. He was dirty and old and not very bright. And I loved him so much. I envied him so much, for he was standing on the threshold of everlasting life. I wanted him to turn his face to God, and not peer back through the smoky light, and stare longingly at this mere preliminary. I said to him: Be glad, be glad. But he did not understand.

His spirit weakened at dawn. It could not mount another day. There were cries of alarm from the family. I took out the necessary properties which I travel in this bag. The vulgar little sins were confessed, absolved, and the man could die. He did so. Brutally, holding on to the last. I spoke my usual words to the family, with my priest's face. My duty was done.

But I could not forget my love for the man.

I came out of the house. I thought I'd walk back, air myself after the death cell. I was very tired. I could hear Saint Peter's bell.

The road was dusty. I remembered the day I came here. I was wearing new shoes. They were white with dust. Do you know, I flicked them over with my stole before being received by the bishop. I was vain and foolish, then. Ambitious, too.

I walked on. They were working in the fields and called to me. I remembered how I loved to work with my hands when I was a boy. But my father said it was unsuitable for one of my birth.

I could see my church in the distance. I was very proud, in a humble way. I thought of my love for the beauty of this not very beautiful place. And I remembered night in the building, with the gold, lit by candlelight, against the darkness.

I thought of you. I remembered you as a friend.

I rested. The country was stretched out. Do you know where the rivers join? I once made love there.

Children came past me. Yes, of course, that's where I got the flowers. I didn't pick them. They were given to me.

I watched the children go. Yes, I was very tired. I could see far beyond the point my eyes could see. Castles, cities, mountains, oceans, plains, forests – and —

And then – oh, my son, my son – and then – I want to tell you —

[*Sewerman* *Do so. Be calm.*]

Grandier My son, I – Am I mad?

Accidental Death of an Anarchist *by Dario Fo (adapted by Alan Cumming and Tim Supple)*

This play is a comic social satire on state and police corruption. Since its first production in Italy in 1970, it has been altered numerous times in many different productions to take account of contemporary events. It is based on a true story about an anarchist arrested for a bombing in Milan in the '60s, who mysteriously plunged through an open fourth floor window on a cold December night while being interrogated by the police. The comedy comes from confusions of identity and the idiocy and lies spun by corrupt policemen around the death of an innocent man.

The action takes place after the publication of an official 'whitewash' about the anarchist's 'accidental' death. In this scene, a madman has been arrested and is being interrogated by the corrupt and bumptious Inspector Bertozzo. This is the Madman's twelfth arrest. His records not only indicate a long record of fraudulent impersonation, but a history of mental illness. As a result, no charges have stuck. On this occasion, he has been arrested for impersonating a psychiatrist, but the Madman has the gift of the gab and is running semantic rings round the thoroughly exasperated Inspector. The Madman is young, intelligent, articulate and completely insane. In an effort to contain him, Bertozzo threatens to put him in handcuffs, but the Madman parries with a firm grasp of the Mental Health Act (learned in a variety of lunatic asylums), and comprehensive knowledge of his rights and the law.

In this speech he outlines his ultimate desire to 'play' a judge, tormenting Bertozzo even more with a manic stream of consciousness and his astute satirical perspective on the judiciary. The Madman is a master of impersonation and disguise and it is for you to decide how far to 'enact' the various characters, from docker to judge, that he describes in this story.

The madness accelerates as the Madman runs rings round the police, while they try to cover their tracks with fabrication and obfuscation, leading them into more and more farcical explanations before the play reaches its 'explosive' finale.

Madman It is my dream to play a judge. But I'm too young. Maybe one day. Because theirs is the best profession of all. At exactly the age when your average, common or garden, ordinary man or woman in the street is being forced out to pasture, a judge is well-groomed and galloping into his prime.

The office worker, fifty-five or sixty, he's getting confused. He thinks the in-tray's the out-tray, forgets to send a memo and costs the company a couple of hundred. Give him a clock, a roll of notes, get him pissed, bye, bye.

The factory worker. She's been on the same part of the assembly line for years. Suddenly all changes. Everything's computerised and all she has to do is press a few buttons and watch a screen. Her eyes hurt, she can't cope. Get someone younger and cheaper in. 'Never mind darling, at least you'll have more time to look after your old man.'

The docker, the miner, the steel-worker – you name it. Body winding down. Tired, sore and slow. Light duties for a while, then the scrap-heap.

And the judge, half-blind, half-crippled, half-senile. Give him a knighthood, a rise in salary and put him in charge of a commission that's going to affect the lives of millions of people. You see old men like peeling cardboard cut-outs, dolled up with insignia, ermine capes, outsize white brillo pads on their heads, looking like pints of luke-warm Guinness, suet-faced, wearing two pairs of glasses on little chains, otherwise they'd lose them. These national treasures exercise a power to destroy or save us with less deliberation than they choose which Chablis to accompany their fish.

'Thirty years for you . . . twenty years for you . . . suspended sentence for you because she was obviously asking for it in that skirt. Six months in an open prison for you because you used to work for Guinness.' They dictate, legislate, sentence, decree. They are sacred, like royalty. Oh yes, I'd love to play that part. One day I will sit in judgement. 'Silence in court. All rise. Oh, Your Honour, you've dropped something. Is this your arse?' 'Thank you, young man. I need that to talk through.'

Inadmissible Evidence *by John Osborne*

This play was first performed at the Royal Court Theatre in 1964. It is set in a dream location – part sterile solicitors' office, part High Court. Its anti-hero Bill Maitland, a promiscuous, boorish lawyer, is in the dock in 'the courtroom of his mind' for 'intending to corrupt the morals of the liege subjects of our Lady the Queen'.

John Maples is one of Maitland's clients in the dream. He is a closet homosexual – a timid, balding young man who is reluctantly married with a six-year-old child. He is described in the stage directions as having 'a quick-witted, improvising nature, not without courage. His flashes of fear are like flashes of creative energy'. He is a southerner who, in spite of his limited education, has made a go of his father-in-law's drapery business in Richmond. Being young was something he missed out on, going from living with his parents to doing National Service. Fresh from the army, he married Hilda after getting her pregnant while drunk. He now finds himself facing prosecution for importuning a plainclothes policeman in a public lavatory. Here he is going over his statement with his solicitor before his trial.

This is part of what is effectively a long confessional speech that is pushed along by Maitland's probing, sometimes prurient questioning. Maples delivers it as if giving evidence, mostly at speed, more polemic than reflection. It is something of a relief to 'spill the beans'. Here he describes his first sexual experience with a casual same-sex partner. The proximity and touch of the body on the train, the journey (going in the right direction!), the following footsteps and the cold draught of air at the station are vividly remembered. So is the dried up dinner he goes back to afterwards – a metaphor for the aridity of his marriage. The actual sexual encounter, notice, is quickly glossed over.

In spite of initial self-disgust, there is danger and excitement in these illicit activities, and relish too at being able to keep them secret from his wife, which of course adds spice. He even managed to keep his big love affair with Denis from her. But it is a secret and a lifestyle that has

65

exhausted him. It is a relief to have been caught. Later he confides that he felt 'better and relaxed' after his arrest, 'as if he was being loved and properly attended to.' It was only when all the implications hit him that he became frightened. Nevertheless, if his dubious solicitor will let him, he wants to plead guilty, 'come out', and finally be free to be who he is.

Maples Sometimes I would think I was unique, of course. You know, years ago. I hoped I was. But I'm not. I'm ordinary. But I wish I wasn't. I didn't have a clue. Nothing happened until after I was married, after Daphne was born. For some reason I got on the wrong train, but it was the right direction more or less and I just stayed on it, standing up, all those bodies pressed together and suddenly I felt two, maybe three, fingers touch me, very lightly. Every time the train stopped more people got out and there was more room. I was scared to look up from my paper and there wasn't any longer any excuse to be so close to anyone. A great draught of air came in from the platform and I felt cold, and it was Gunnersbury Station which is not too far from me, so I looked up and got out. I didn't dare look back but I heard the footsteps behind me. That was the first time and I'd had a few drinks first and I was very cold, at the back of some row of shops called something Parade, by the Midland Bank. About half past seven at night. That's about all I remember of it. When I got in, my dinner was all overcooked and simmering on a plate over the gas stove with the gravy gone hard round the edge of the plate, which is a bit like the way Hilda does things, spills them or upsets them or does them too much and she wasn't feeling well and couldn't get the baby to sleep. I went out into the garden, put my fingers down my throat and then buried it all with a trowel. If I wasn't married I'd have done it all the time, one to another, I suppose, but I don't think so. That's never been what I wanted. Oh, not that I haven't behaved. . . . They're right to get me, people like me. There was a young fellow, a sales manager at a store in Kingston. Do you know what I did? He was married. Nice girl.

Rather attractive, not long married. Well, I set my sights and one night the three of us went out, got drunk, and while, all the time, while his wife was out in the front —

[**Bill** *Driving?* –

Maples *Driving* –

Bill *Actually in the back?*]

Maples And she never knew. We were so damned sharp, she never knew from beginning to end. Still doesn't know. Like Hilda, she never knew about Denis, about giving him up. I gave him up, you see. He wanted me to leave Hilda and take on a new life altogether. He begged me. He threatened to phone up or write to me. But he hasn't. He kept his promise. I longed to break the whole thing, and I think I would have done this particular night.

*[The dialogue is cut here, to resume with **Maples** – ed.]*

I knew it was going to happen. Sounds camp, but then the truth so often is. He was quite young, younger than I am, with lots of fair, wavy hair, like mine used to be, when I just went in the Army, before I met Hilda, before it started to go; he looked up. In the usual way. His eyes were pale and his cheekbones looked sharp and frail as if you could have smashed them with a knock from your finger, but when he walked away, you could see how really strong he must be. He walked straight into the cottage at number one entrance, you know, by the Regent Palace. And that was it. There was another one in there and they both of them grabbed me. Savile Row Station. Oh, quite gently. And no surprise to any of us. Denis and I had often talked about it happening. They seemed nice enough at first. I began to feel better and relaxed, as if I was being loved openly and attended on, and then, then the pressure turned on. What I ought to do. What the magistrate would say. What they knew. The one who had asked for the light had seen me with Denis. He said they knew all about him. About both of us. I had to keep him out of it. I knew nothing could be worse. So I, I signed this statement. And there it is. In front of you.

Justice *by John Galsworthy*

This is perhaps Galsworthy's most famous play. It's theme
is prison reform and the cruelty of the criminal justice
system in Victorian England. It received its first production
at the Duke of York's Theatre in 1910. Act 2 takes place in
the Court of Justice. There are several other long courtroom
speeches in it, which you might find useful.

This is the story of William Falder, a young clerk in a
lawyer's office, whose life is destroyed by the legal system.
Falder steals ninety pounds from his employer and runs off
with the woman he loves to save her and her children from
a brutal husband. However, he is captured and brought to
court where, in spite of this robust defence, he is convicted
and sentenced to three years in prison. On his release he is
a broken man and everything conspires against him. The
woman he loves resorts to prostitution and he is arrested
again for working with forged references. Rather than go
back to prison, he kills himself – a victim of Victorian moral
values.

In this scene the Crown has just presented its evidence
and Frome, Falder's counsel, is opening the case for the
defence. Frome is described in the stage directions as a
'young, tall man, clean–shaved, in a very white wig,' but this
is certainly not prescriptive! He is upper-class, educated
(almost certainty Oxbridge), radical, compassionate, urbane,
practised and highly articulate.

He uses his considerable adversarial skill to appeal to the
jury. He makes no attempt to insult them by disputing
Falder's guilt, but pleads that the crime was committed
while his client's mind was temporarily disturbed. He cites
Falder's inexperience and youth, appealing to their
understanding and compassion for a young man in love
with noble, if misguided motives. He paints a moving
picture of the young woman's desperate plight. Should they
condemn this young man to prison and destroy the rest of
his life for a moment of weakness? Faced with the dilemma
of either seeing the woman he loved brutalised, or taking
the law into his own hands, what choice did he have?
Frome's arguments are powerful and persuasive – enough to

melt the hardest heart and challenge the most deeply rooted prejudice.

Look at this speech in the context of the moral framework of late Victorian England, where a working-class woman was wholly dependent on her husband, divorce was out of the question and the consequences of legal separation too dire to contemplate.

———————————

Frome (*rising and bowing to the* **Judge**) If it pleases your lordship and members of the jury. I am not going to dispute the fact that the prisoner altered this cheque, but I am going to put before you evidence as to the condition of his mind, and to submit that you would not be justified in finding that he was responsible for his actions at the time. I am going to show you, in fact, that he did this in a moment of aberration, amounting to temporary insanity, caused by the violent distress under which he was labouring. Gentlemen, the prisoner is only twenty-three years old. I shall call before you a woman from whom you will learn the events that led up to this act. You will hear more from her own lips the tragic circumstances of her life, the still more tragic infatuation with which she has inspired the prisoner. This woman, gentlemen, has been leading a miserable existence with a husband who habitually ill-uses her, from whom she actually goes in terror of her life. I am not, of course, saying that it's either right or desirable for a young man to fall in love with a married woman, or that it's his business to rescue her from an ogre-like husband. I'm not saying anything of the sort. But we all know the power of the passion of love; and I would ask you to remember, gentlemen, in listening to her evidence, that, married to a drunken and violent husband, she has no power to get rid of him; for, as you know, another offence besides violence is necessary to enable a woman to obtain a divorce; and of this offence it does not appear that her husband is guilty.

[*Judge* *Is this relevant, Mr. Frome?*

Frome *My lord, I submit extremely – I shall be able to show your lordship that directly.*

Judge *Very well.*]

Frome In these circumstances, what alternatives were left to her? She could either go on living with this drunkard, in terror of her life; or she could apply to the Court for a separation order. Well, gentlemen, my experience of such cases assures me that this would have given her very insufficient protection from the violence of such a man; and even if effectual would very likely have reduced her either to the workhouse or the streets – for it's not easy, as she is now finding, for an unskilled woman without means of livelihood to support herself and her children without resorting either to the Poor Law or – to speak quite plainly – to the sale of her body.

[*Judge You are ranging rather far, Mr Frome.*

Frome *I shall fire point blank in a minute, my lord.*

Judge Let us hope so.]

Frome Now, gentlemen, mark – and this is what I have been leading up to – this woman will tell you, and the prisoner will confirm her, that, confronted with such alternatives, she set her whole hopes on himself, knowing the feeling with which she had inspired him. She saw a way out of her misery by going with him to a new country, where they would both be unknown, and might pass as husband and wife. This was a desperate and, as my friend Mr. Cleaver will no doubt call it, an immoral resolution; but, as a fact, the minds of both of them were constantly turned towards it. One wrong is no excuse for another, and those who are never likely to be faced by such a situation possibly have the right to hold up their hands – as to that I prefer to say nothing. But whatever view you take, gentlemen, of this part of the prisoner's story – whatever opinion you form of the right of these two young people under such circumstances to take the law into their own hands – the fact remains that this young woman in her distress, and this young man, little more than a boy, who was so devotedly attached to her, *did* conceive this – if you like – reprehensible design of going away together. Now, for that, of course, they required money, and – they had none. As to the actual events of the morning of July 7th, on which this cheque was altered, the events on which I rely to prove the defendant's irresponsibility – I shall allow those events to speak for themselves, through the lips of my witnesses. Robert Cokeson. (*He turns, looks round, takes up a sheet of paper, and waits.*)

The Hairy Ape *by Eugene O'Neill*

This unsettling early one-act play was first performed at the Playwright's Theatre, New York in 1922. It is an experimental mix of expressionism and naturalism – a parable about class conflict. Like all O'Neill's work it is deeply autobiographical and rooted in his own life-long search for a sense of belonging.

Robert Smith – 'Yank' – is a hulk of a man – a crude, hard-drinking, tough talking, muscular, hairy-chested coal-stoker from The Bronx who works in the stoke-hole of an American transatlantic liner. He relishes the work – coal-dust is fresh air to him. He gives the orders and others jump. He's a kind of 'everyman' as his name 'Bob Smith' and nickname implies – a representative of society's disaffected masses who understands his place in the order of things. His natural home is the coal-caked bowels of the ship – that is until the pampered 'do gooder' Mildred Douglas – daughter of the wealthy owner of the Line – deigns to visit the baking stoke hole to see 'how the other half lives'.

Confronted by a scene from 'hell' and horrified by the brutality of the men, she faints and Yank begins to see himself as society might see him. A hairy ape at the bottom of the social heap. Driven by the fact that his labour underpins Mildred's privilege, and obsessed by the thought of joining the world she represents, Yank goes to New York with his mate to take revenge. But soon he is in prison for causing a fracas amongst churchgoers on Fifth Avenue, and thrown out of the offices of a radical worker's union as 'a capitalist spy.' Rejected on all fronts Yank seeks solace amongst 'the hairy apes' in the zoo.

This is a section from the last speech of the play. Yank is chatting to an enormous gorilla. He has lost his connection with the past, but can't find a route into any other way of being. In this bitter monologue Yank struggles for a sense of belonging. He is ill-designed to cope with anything outside the world he knows, but if not a cog in society's machine, what is he? Bewildered by the confusion in his brain, Yank wrestles with the conundrum of being a member of the human race but finding no way to play any part in it. He

identifies with the gigantic caged animal – but even the
gorilla seems more at home in his world than Yank feels he
can ever be. When he finally sets the gorilla free, it crushes
him to death, throws him in the cage and slams the door.
'And perhaps' moots O'Neill in his final stage directions,
'the Hairy Ape at last belongs'.

Yank (*with a hard, bitter laugh*) Welcome to your city, huh? Hail,
hail, de gang's all here! (*At the sound of his voice the chattering dies
away into an attentive silence.* **Yank** *walks up to the gorilla's cage and,
leaning over the railing, stars in at its occupant, who stares back at him,
silent and motionless. There is a pause of dead stillness. Then* **Yank**
*begins to talk in a friendly, confidential tone, half-mockingly, but with a
deep undercurrent of sympathy.*) Say, yuh're some hard-lookin' guy,
ain't yuh? I seen lots of tough nuts dat de gang called gorillas, but
yuh're de foist real one I ever seen. Some chest yuh got, and
shoulders, and dem arms and mits! I bet yuh got a punch in eider
fist dat'd knock 'em silly! (*This with genuine admiration. The gorilla, as
if he understood, stands upright, swelling out his chest and pounding on it
with his fist.* **Yank** *grins sympathetically.*) Sure, I get yuh. Yuh
challenge de whole woild, huh? Yuh got what I was sayin' even if
yuh muffed de woids. (*Then bitterness creeping in.*) And why wouldn't
yuh get me? Ain't we both members of de same club – de Hairy
Apes? (*They stare at each other – a pause – then* **Yank** *goes on slowly
and bitterly.*) So yuh're what she seen when she looked at me, de
white-faced tart! I was you to her, get me? On'y outa de cage – broke
out – free to moider her, see? Sure! Dat's what she tought. She
wasn't wise dat I was in a cage, too – worser'n yours – sure – a damn
sight – 'cause you got some chanct to bust loose – but me – (*He
grows confused.*) Aw hell! It's all wrong, ain't it? (*A pause.*) I s'pose
yuh wanter know what I'm doin' here, huh? I been warmin' a bench
down to de Battery – ever since last night. Sure. I seen de sun come
up. Dat was pretty, too – all red and pink and green. I was lookin' at
de skyscrapers – steel – and all de ships comin' in, sailin' out, all
over de oith – and dey was steel, too. De sun was warm, dey wasn't

74

no clouds, and dere was a breeze blowin'. Sure, it was great stuff. I got it aw right – what Paddy said about dat bein' de right dope – on'y I couldn't get *in* it, see? I couldn't belong in dat. It was over my head. And I kept tinkin' – and den I beat it up here to see what youse was like. And I waited till dey was all gone to git yuh alone. Say, how d'yuh feel sittin' in dat pen all de time, havin' to stand for 'em comin' and starin' at yuh – de white-faced, skinny tarts and de boobs what marry 'em – makin' fun of yuh, laughin' at yuh, gittin' scared of yuh – damn 'em! (*He pounds on the rail with his fist. The gorilla rattles the bars of his cage and snarls. All the other monkeys set up an angry chattering in the darkness.* **Yank** *goes on excitedly.*) Sure! Dat's de way it hits me, too. On'y yuh're lucky, see? Yuh don't belong wit 'em and yuh know it. But me, I belong wit 'em – but I don't, see? Dey don't belong wit me, dat's what. Get me? Tinkin' is hard – (*He passes one hand across his forehead with a painful gesture. The gorilla growls impatiently.* **Yank** *goes on gropingly.*) It's dis way, what I'm drivin' at. Youse can sit and dope dream in de past, green woods, de jungle and de rest of it. Den yuh belong and dey don't. Den yuh kin laugh at 'em see? Yuh're de champ of de woild. But me – I ain't got no past to tink in, nor nothin' dat's comin', on'y what's now – and dat don't belong. Sure, you're de best off! Yuh can't tink, can yuh? Yuh can't talk neider. But I kin make a bluff at talkin' and tinkin' – a'most git away wit it – a'most! – and dat's where de joker comes in. (*He laughs.*) I ain't on oith and I ain't in Heaven, get me? I'm in de middle tryin' to separate 'em, takin' all de woist punches from bot' of 'em. Maybe dat's what dey call Hell, uh? But you, yuh're at de bottom. You belong! Sure! Yuh're de on'y one in de woild dat does, yuh lucky stiff!

Oh What a Lovely War *by Joan Littlewood, Charles Chilton and Theatre Workshop*

This play is a satire on the realities of the First Word War told through songs, dramatised primary source material and horrifying battle statistics. It was first performed by Joan Littlewood's Theatre Workshop at the Theatre Royal in Stratford East in 1963 – an alternative theatre production that reached the West End and was made into a hugely popular film in 1969. A small cast plays a variety of roles, quick-changing from soldiers to nation states, nurses to mill girls, in a company-devised piece that continues to remind us of the horror and waste of war.

In this sequence a sergeant major is instructing his raw recruits on bayonet drill. He is the stereotypical drill sergeant. Working class. Rough and ready. Bullying. Not officer material and resenting anyone who looks as if they might be! He's in charge. He has no respect for the recruits. He can be as abusive, domineering and patronising, as he likes. He's performed this drill many times before. Same language. Same jokes. It has become something of a performance therefore. Look at the stage directions: 'he speaks in an incomprehensible garbled language'. The speech is delivered with great rapidity in a demented and manic gibberish. You'll need to practice your tongue twisters to get your tongue round this one! Only the phrases printed in italics are comprehensible and these should be delivered with particular vitriol in the ear of the chosen victim.

The sense of the piece is articulated through the sergeant major's actions, manner and attitudes, not from what we actually hear of what he says. His agenda is to teach the recruits how to become killing machines and he enacts the bloodthirsty scenarios of killing and maiming the enemy with savage and realistic commitment. Done well, this speech should be a showy tour de force.

Bayonet Drill Sequence: The soldiers go off, leaving the recruits. A sergeant-major enters and instructs them in bayonet drill. He speaks in an incomprehensible garbled language. What he says is roughly as follows. Occasional words can be made out and these are printed in italics:

Now, you lousy lot, we're going to learn rifle drill and bayonet practice. I'm going to teach you how to handle a rifle and fix bayonets. – Your rifle is your best friend and I'm going to be your worst bloody enemy. First thing, get your rifle on your left shoulder, left hand parallel to the ground, right hand down the seam of your trousers. First move your right hand smartly across your body, grabbing the rifle at the point of balance, and bring your rifle down between your knees. You at the end there I'll have your bloody *guts* for *garters* in a minute. Now then, with the rifle in that position you come to the bayonet fix. BAYONET!! FIX!! With right hand hold rifle six inches from the top, the first six inches don't count. Right – BAYONET – ONE! TWO – bring bayonet down at angle of ninety degrees over the rifle and THREE bring the bayonet down over the bayonet catch. BAYONET . . . Wait for it . . . Bayonet, by numbers, one – two – three – Fix.

One recruit cannot find his bayonet – the Sergeant-Major approaches him.

Hello, hello, hello, hello. Where's your bayonet?

He swears in the recruit's ear. During this, the recruit's rifle has slipped between his knees.

Where's your bloody rifle – gone now? Standing on parade like some fancy *fairy!*

He pulls the rifle out from between the recruit's legs and the recruit places the bayonet quickly on his rifle.

Now then, next position is the lunge. Bring the rifle up smartly. Right hand on the neck of the butt, left hand at the point of balance, left foot forward. Right hand behind butt of rifle to give it a thrust. In – out – on guard! and don't poke about there like you're poking a bleeding fire either. Now get your right foot firmly balanced or you'll fall flat on your arse. Now when he's coming at you with a lunge – 'cos he's also joined the bleedin' army – you can do what we call the *left parry*. Which is – get the rifle under the swivel butt with the left hand, and don't bloody ask me what the swivel butt is here for. Get the right hand under butt of rifle, and swing over to the left and bash his head in and if that doesn't work, swing into the right parry. Now the right parry is getting the rifle at the point of balance in the left hand – get the right hand on the butt of the rifle and swing into his balls. *Ruin his chances*, and then on, 'cos there's plenty more where he just came from. Now let's start with the right parry. Right parry, by numbers, by the count of three – one – two – three! Come on, get that butt in there. Right, you dress back, you dress back, you dress back . . . You again.

The recruit on the end does it appallingly. The Sergeant-Major beckons the recruit over to him, and starts a tirade.

You're *bloody clever*, you're *bloody smart* you are. I've been in the *Army twenty-five bloody years*, and got *three bloody stripes* to prove it. I suppose you've been to *public school*. And you don't go forward with all those *bloody lah-de-dah and tally-ho's*. You go like this.

The Sergeant does right parry, accompanied by a frightening blood-curdling scream. He orders the recruit to do the same, three times in succession, the recruit screaming and getting very excited.

That's better. Fall in, all of you. I've got eyes in the back of my bloody head. I'm keeping a fatherly eye on you. Right then – get to your positions for bayonet charge, and get that look on your face. You just think of *those bastards out there. Oh my God, look at that!*

Drawing attention to the recruits' insipid faces.

Think of those bastards out there. Up your *mother*, up your *sister*, up your *brother*, too, by the look of some of you. Platoon by numbers – bayonet! —

Notices recruit's position.

What you got, a bleeding *bow and arrow* there? CHARGE!

Eden Cinema *by Marguerite Duras*
(translated by Barbara Bray)

This play was adapted by Marguerite Duras from her third
novel *Un Barrage contre le Pacifique*. It was first produced by
the Renaud-Barrault Company in Paris in 1977. This is a
complex play about memory and the destructive power of
love based on Duras' own experiences of growing up in
colonial French Indo-China. It is a stylised, retrospective
piece in which the characters reveal their inner lives directly
to the audience while also participating in the action.

The Mother, a French widow, is cheated out of her
savings when she invests in a worthless tract of flooding salt
plain on the west coast of Cambodia. Her struggle against
poverty and her efforts to protect her rice paddies by
erecting walls to hold back the Pacific, provide a powerful
metaphor for her futile attempts to hold her family
together.

Her children, Joseph and Suzanne, are trapped by The
Mother and their circumstances. They are the narrators of
their mother's story. It begins with her purchase of the bad
land in 1924, and follows the family fortunes until The
Mother's death. As the story unravels, family tensions are
laid bare.

A rich admirer has given Suzanne a valuable diamond.
The family try to sell it in the city, to raise money for a sea
wall, but the diamond is flawed and worth only half what
they had hoped. The Mother's crazy and irrational attempts
to raise the full price for the stone have driven Joseph away.
Now he has come back with an extraordinary story.

Here, he talks to Suzanne who lies some distance from
him on the riverbank. He has decided to go away again. He
describes how he sold the diamond for the full price, but
managed to keep it as well. As he recalls the intimate
exchanges of his meeting with the woman in the darkened
Eden Cinema, and the almost filmic aftermath, he isn't
really talking to Suzanne but to himself. The story is
sparsely and evocatively told in short simple sentences,
with gaps where he can't quite remember. It is imbued with
a kind of wonder that such amazing things could have

happened to him. This is the experience that releases him
from the thrall of The Mother and enables him to leave her
and the flood plain for the last time.

———————————

Joseph It happened at the Eden Cinema. One evening. She arrived
late. I didn't notice her at first. There was a man with her. I think I
saw him first. Suddenly I heard very heavy breathing, right next to
me. It was him. She saw me looking at him and turned towards me.
She smiled. She said: 'It's always like this.' I said: 'Always?' She said:
'Yes, always.' I asked her who he was. She laughed. She said he was
her husband. She took out a packet of cigarettes from her bag.
Players 555. She asked for a light. I gave her one.

Pause.

I saw her hands. Her eyes. She was looking at me. Her hand was very
slim and supple. (*Pause.*) It felt almost as if the bones were broken.
We didn't talk any more. I don't know how long it went on. The
lights were going up. I let go of her hand. But it sought mine again.
I thought I'd leave. But I couldn't. I said to myself, she must be used
to picking men like this in cinema. The lights went up. Her hand
was withdrawn. I didn't dare look at her. She, yes, she dared – she
looked at me. The man had suddenly woken up. I thought he was
rather good looking. She pointed me out to him. She said: 'He's a
hunter from Réam.' We'd left the cinema. I was just behind her.
They went up to an eight-cylinder Delage. The man turned round,
said to me: 'Are you coming?' I said: 'Yes.'

Music. The Eden Cinema Waltz.

We stopped at a night-club. 'We'll have a whisky,' said the man. It
was then I understood. When he had that whisky. We left that club.
Went on to another one near the port. Had more to drink. And so it
went on. And on. Suddenly, it was morning. I asked myself what I
was doing there, with those people. It was six o'clock in the
morning. The man had fallen asleep with his head on the table. She

leaned towards me, stretching over him. We kissed. I felt as if I'd died. I'm rather hazy about what happened next. I remember there were gardens round the night-club, waterfalls, swimming pools. Everything was . . . very light . . . and empty . . . emptied . . . I drove the Delage. We went to a hotel. We stayed there for a week. Once she asked me to tell her about my life. I told her about the diamond. She told me to fetch it. Said she'd buy it. When I got back to the Central Hotel I found it in my pocket, together with the money.

Travesties *by Tom Stoppard*

This is an absurdist farce based on a true story and peopled with historical figures who were all living in neutral Switzerland during the First World War. According to Stoppard's introduction, the Irish writer James Joyce was approached by Claude Sykes, an actor living in Zurich at the time, about forming a theatre company to mount plays in English. Their first production was to be *The Importance of Being Ernest*. Henry Carr, an insignificant consular official and amateur actor, was approached to play Algernon.

Carr is Stoppard's narrator, who appears as an old man looking back on his life. He takes us through memories featuring Lenin, the eccentric Dadaist artist Tristan Tzara, and James Joyce whom he sued for both slander and the reimbursement for the cost of Algernon's trousers! These characters' wildly differing views on the relationship between politics and art provides the play's comic framework.

James Joyce is a Dubliner who is articulate, showy, self-opinionated, convinced of his own genius and, at the time this play is set, aged thirty-six. Earlier in this scene, Tristan Tzara and Joyce have confronted each other about the nature and purpose of art. Tzara pours scorn on traditional values, which he thinks are represented by Joyce, rejecting everything that presents art and artists as anything but nonsense. He demonstrates his disdain by smashing any crockery that comes to hand.

Unimpressed, Joyce responds to his outburst with this cutting and dismissive 'put down', discrediting Tzara's talents, trumpeting the artist's noble calling, and arrogantly asserting the enduring genius of his own work as evidenced by his proposed reinterpretation of Homer's *Odyssey* – *Ulysses*. He dismisses Tzara's work as 'fashionable magic', exiting with a flamboyant Irish farewell.

Although James Joyce is a real literary figure whose life you can research, remember that his character here is coloured by Carr's prejudicial memories of him. It will help to take account of his less than flattering descriptions of Joyce throughout the play!

Joyce You are an over-excited little man, with a need for self-expression far beyond the scope of your natural gifts. This is not discreditable. Neither does it make you an artist. An artist is the magician put among men to gratify – capriciously – their urge for immortality. The temples are built and brought down around him, continuously and contiguously, from Troy to the fields of Flanders. If there is any meaning in any of it, it is in what survives as art, yes even in the celebration of tyrants, yes even in the celebration of nonentities. What now of the Trojan War if it had been passed over by the artist's touch? Dust. A forgotten expedition prompted by Greek merchants looking for new markets. A minor redistribution of broken pots. But it is we who stand enriched, by a tale of heroes, of a golden apple, a wooden horse, a face that launched a thousand ships – and above all, of Ulysses, the wanderer, the most human, the most complete of all heroes – husband, father, son, lover, farmer, soldier, pacifist, politician, inventor and adventurer . . . It is a theme so overwhelming that I am almost afraid to treat it. And yet I with my Dublin Odyssey will double that immortality, yes by God *there's* a corpse that will dance for some time yet and *leave the world precisely as it finds it* – and if you hope to shame it into the grave with your fashionable magic, I would strongly advise you to try and acquire some genius and if possible some subtlety before the season is quite over. Top o' the morning, Mr. Tzara!

A Man for All Seasons *by Robert Bolt*

This play was first performed in London in 1962. It dramatises the conflict between Henry VIII and his Lord Chancellor, Sir Thomas More, who refused to acknowledge the legitimacy of Henry's divorce from Catherine of Aragon and marriage to Anne Boleyn. It explores issues of conscience and the confrontation between church and state.

Sir Thomas is a devout man who cannot, in good conscience, sanction Henry's actions. He has taken refuge in silence rather than give his approval. Every pressure has been used to persuade him to submit, yet he remains intransigent and refuses to acknowledge either the marriage or Henry's self-appointment as supreme head of the Church of England to facilitate it. For this he is imprisoned in The Tower and arraigned at Westminster Hall to answer a charge of High Treason. The punishment is death.

Thomas Cromwell is one of the King's Secretaries and Sir Thomas' chief accuser in the court. He is in his late thirties, an intellectual bully, sycophantic, clever, conspiratorial and ruthless. The stage directions describe him as 'subtle and serious; the face expressing not inner tension but the tremendous outgoing will of the Renaissance. A self-conceit that can cradle gross crimes in the name of effective action'.

He is addressing the jury in the tones of 'prosecuting council'. Although the law states that 'Silence gives consent', Cromwell is at pains to persuade the Jury that in this case it means otherwise. It is a shoddy line of reasoning delivered with adversarial skill that scarcely masks his loathing for Sir Thomas and everything he stands for. He knows that as long as Sir Thomas remains alive, the King's conscience will continue to trouble him; yet if Cromwell brings about his death, the King will scapegoat him to avoid responsibility. He is in a cleft stick.

Pragmatically, despite his loathing, the only safe course open to him is to persuade Sir Thomas to say what the King wants to hear. It is quite beyond him that a man should place his conscience before his life, or his God before his duty and his King.

Cromwell Now, Sir Thomas, you stand upon your silence.

[*More* I do.

Cromwell But,] Gentlemen of the Jury, there are many kinds of silence. Consider first the silence of a man when he is dead. Let us say we go into the room where he is lying; and let us say it is in the dead of night – there's nothing like darkness for sharpening the ear; and we listen. What do we hear? Silence. What does it betoken, this silence? Nothing. This is silence, pure and simple. But consider another case. Suppose I were to draw a dagger from my sleeve and make to kill the prisoner with it, and suppose their lordships there, instead of crying out for me to stop or crying out for help to stop me, maintained their silence. That *would* betoken! It would betoken a willingness that I should do it, and under the law they would be guilty with me. So silence can, according to circumstances, speak. Consider, now, the circumstances of the prisoner's silence. The oath was put to good and faithful subjects up and down the country and they had declared His Grace's Title to be just and good. And when it came to the prisoner he refused. He calls this silence. Yet is there a man in this court, is there a man in this country, who does not *know* Sir Thomas More's opinion of this title? Of course not! But how can that be? Because this silence betokened – nay this silence *was* – not silence at all, but most eloquent denial.

The Weavers *by Gerhart Hauptmann (translated by Frank Marcus)*

This play is about a rebellion against the mechanisms of the Industrial Revolution. Credited as being the first 'socialist' drama, it dramatises the true story of the uprising of starving peasant weavers in the Silesian mountains in 1844. Their rebellion against exploitative employers was hopelessly disorganised and crushed by the military. The play broke new ground in as much as rather than the protagonist being an individual, the oppressed weavers – members of the peasant class – are the protagonists of the play.

Hauptmann came from a family of weavers so understood the deprivations of their world, although their circumstances had changed by 1893 when he was writing this. *The Weavers* is considered his masterpiece and brought him fame as the leading playwright of his generation.

Herr Dreissiger is a manufacturer in his early forties, who buys his finished articles from a fragile cottage industry. He is stern, hard-hearted, self-interested, brutal, obese and asthmatic. He is loathed by the weavers for the way he treats them. Act 1 takes place in his office where a dismal crowd of men, women and children have come for their wages. They have been waiting for hours, but are given short shrift by Dreissiger's manager, Pfeifer, who humiliates and underpays them.

A militant weaver, Baeker, dares to complain about their treatment and demand his full pay, incurring Dreissiger's wrath. When a little boy complains of being hungry and faints in the crowd Dreissiger affects sympathy. But careless of his own responsibility for the child's sickly condition, he blames the parents and threatens to reject work from children in future, or give up the business altogether, driving more nails in the peasant's coffin. He presents himself and the 'hard-done-by' manufacturers as the exploited ones. Why can't they understand the difficulties he has to face? He claims to be the weavers' benefactor, characterising his situation as hopeless, because he can't sell their badly manufactured goods. In reality he and his underlings thrive on the labour of the peasants, spending more on cigars in a day than a family earns in a week!

The weavers are too starved, subdued and terrorised to disagree. And Dreissiger knows they don't have any other options.

Dreissiger It was nothing serious. The child is quite bright again. (*Excited, walking about, puffing.*) But it's still a disgrace. The child is like a blade of grass waiting to be blown over. It's inconceivable how people . . . how parents can be so irresponsible. Burdening him with two bundles of cotton on a good one and a half mile walk – it's really hard to credit. I'll simply have to make it a rule that no products will be accepted from children. (*He paces about again in silence.*) Anyway I shall insist that such a thing doesn't happen again. Who gets blamed for it in the end? The factory owners, of course. It's always our fault. If some poor little boy gets trapped in the snow in the winter and falls asleep, some hack will come running and two days later we'll read a horror-story in all the papers. The father, the parents who sent out such a child . . . it's never their fault! Oh no, it's the factory owner who's the scapegoat. The weavers are always handled with velvet gloves, but it's the factory owner who gets it in the neck: he's a man with a heart of stone, a dangerous fellow who's fair game for any press-hound that wants to take a bite. He lives in luxury and pleasure and pays the poor weavers starvation wages. It never occurs to them that such a man has also got worries and sleepless nights; that he runs great risks undreamt of by the workers; that he sometimes doesn't know whether he's coming or going with all that addition, division and multiplication; doing his calculations again and again; that he's got to think of a hundred different things and always, as it were, fighting matters of life and death; he has so much competition that not a day passes without aggravation and loss: they don't make a song-and-dance about that. And who doesn't depend on the factory-owner, who doesn't suck him dry and want to live off him!

No, no! You should be in his shoes sometimes, you'd soon get fed up. (*After some reflection.*) Remember how that ruffian, that lout Baecker, carried on just now! Now he'll go and trumpet that I'm God knows how pitiless. How I kick the weavers out over any little thing. Is that true? Am I so heartless?

Several voices: 'No, Herr Dreissiger!'

That's what I think too. And then these scabs march around singing nasty songs about us factory-owners; they talk about hunger but have enough to drink their liquor by the quart. They ought to stick their noses in somewhere else and smell the conditions of the linen-weavers. They can talk about hardship. But you people, you cotton-weavers, the way things are with you, you should quietly thank God. And I ask the old, industrious and efficient weavers who are here: can a worker who knows his trade make a living with me or not?

Very many voices: 'Yes, Herr Dreissiger.'

You see! – A man like Baecker wouldn't understand this. But I advise you, keep those louts in check. If things get too hot I'll quit. I'll give up the business and then you'll see what's what. Then you'll see who gives you work. Certainly not the honourable Baecker.

The Quare Fellow *by Brendan Behan*

This play was first produced in the tiny Pike Theatre in Dublin in 1954, then produced by Joan Littlewood's Theatre Workshop two years later before transferring to the West End.

It is the blackest and most poignant of comedies about judicial hanging; a vibrant, rumbustuous, unsentimental mix of strong language, humour, drama, social comment, rage, poetry and song set in an Irish prison in 1947. It takes place during the tense hours before a hanging. Capital punishment was still practised in Ireland and Britain and was the subject of heated debate. Although this was one of the first plays to oppose it, it is not a piece of propaganda but an insight into prison life and the effect capital punishment had on both warders and inmates alike. It is rooted in Behan's own experiences of imprisonment for republican activities in the 1940s.

'The quare fellow' of the title, ('quare' is prison slang for condemned prisoner) has butchered his brother and awaits his fate. Although he is the central character in the play, he never appears.

Warden Regan is a prison warder in his middle years. He is a charitable, merciful Catholic with a black sense of humour, who does his job with fairness and compassion. He has attended many hangings – the condemned all ask for him – and is to be present at this one too. It is not something he ever gets used to. He opposes the barbarity of the system but does his duty in the most humane way he can.

In this speech he is talking to Crimmin, a new young warder who 'the quare fellow' has also asked to be there. They have been overseeing the digging of the grave and are waiting for the Hangman to come to measure the prisoner for the 'drop'. It is Crimmin's first hanging. He is anxious about it as he has never seen anyone die before. He expresses his anxiety to Regan who responds by telling him about his own first experience.

With fatherly concern, Regan tries to reassure Crimmin about the terrible task that lies ahead. He impresses on him the importance of the duty he is about to perform and how he must temper duty with compassion in the condemned man's last minutes on earth.

_____

Warder Regan I don't like it now any more than I did the first time.

[*Crimmin No sir.*]

Warder Regan It was a little Protestant lad, the first time; he asked if he could be walked backwards into the hanghouse so as he wouldn't see the rope.

[*Crimmin God forgive them.*]

[*Warder Regan May He forgive us all.*] The young clergyman that was on asked if the prison chaplain could accompany him; it was his first hanging too. I went to the Canon to ask him, a fine big man he was. 'Regan,' he says, 'I thought I was going to escape it this time, but you never escape. I don't suppose neither of us ever will. Ah well,' he says, 'maybe being hung twenty times will get me out of purgatory a minute or two sooner.'

[*Crimmin Amen, a Thighearna Dhia.*]

Warder Regan The young clergyman was great; he read a bit of the Bible to the little Protestant lad while they waited and he came in with him, holding his hand and telling him, in their way, to lean on God's mercy that was stronger than the power of men. I walked beside them and guided the boy on to the trap and under the beam. The rope was put round him and the washer under his ear and the hood pulled over his face. And still the young clergyman called out to him, in a grand steady voice, in through the hood: 'I declare to you, my living Christ this night . . .' and he stroked his head till he went down. Then he fainted; the Canon and myself had to carry him out to the Governor's office.

A pause. We are aware of the men working at the grave.

The quare fellow asked for you especially, Crimmin; he wanted you because you're a young lad, not yet practised in badness. You'll be a consolation to him in the morning when he's surrounded by a crowd of bigger bloody ruffians than himself, if the truth were but told. He's depending on you, and you're going to do your best for him.

Play with a Tiger *by Doris Lessing*

This play was first produced at the Comedy Theatre in 1962. It is about the battle of the sexes and is set in the emerging post-war classless society of 1958. Lessing was one of the first writers to put women's issues at the centre of her work.

The play takes place over a long night in the life of Australian expat Anna Freeman. Anna is a thirty-five-year-old widow with a young son who works on the 'artistic fringes' as a writer in inner city London. She and Dave love each other but are unsuited to marriage because neither is prepared to conform to society's stereotypes or make the necessary compromises for their relationship to work.

Dave is an American expat aged thirty-three. He is mercurial, spirited, articulate, amusing, 'a bit nuts', engaging, promiscuous, and 'rootless on principal'. He dresses sloppily and wears his hair in a fashionable crew cut. He loves Anna, but is 'not prepared to be any woman's pet'. Anna has recently discovered that Dave has got a conventional young American girl pregnant, but this is a card she holds close to her chest until the end of the play.

In Act 2, the naturalistic style of the play deconstructs into something more experimental as Anna and Dave regress into past lives, explaining and re-enacting how their natures and attitudes have been formed as they struggle to establish a blueprint for their relationship.

Here Dave is describing a visit to a psychoanalyst, made when he was a young man. He is making Anna laugh with his humorous and colourful storytelling, switching seamlessly between the po-faced Oxbridge English of Doctor Melville Cooper-Anstey and his own Chicago drawl. It is quite a performance! But it has at its heart his desire for Anna to open herself up to him, a disdain for conformity and the privilege of the English upper-classes, and questions about the malaise at the heart of the American dream. And for all the humour, we sense his quest to give his life a meaning that has somehow eluded him.

Dave It was no laughing matter. I talked for one hour by the clock, begging and pleading for the favour of one constructive word from him. But he merely sat like this, and then he said: 'I'll see you next Thursday, at five o'clock precisely.' I said, it was no laughing matter – for a whole week I was in a trance, waiting for the ultimate revelation – you know how we all live, waiting for that revelation? Then I danced up to his room and lay on to his couch and lay waiting. He said not a word. Finally I said don't think I'm resisting you, doc, please don't think it. Talk doc, I said. Give. Let yourself go. Then the hour was nearly up. I may say, I'd given him a thumb-nail sketch of my life previously. He spoke at last: 'Tell me, Mr Miller, how many jobs did you say you had had?' My God, doc, I said, nearly falling over myself in my eagerness to oblige, if I knew, I'd tell you. 'You would admit,' he said at last, 'that the pattern of your life shows, ho, hum, ha, a certain instability?' My God, yes, doc, I said, panting at his feet, that's it, you're on to it, hold fast to it doc, that's the word, instability. Now give doc, give. Tell me, why is it that a fine upstanding American boy like me, with all the advantages our rich country gives its citizens, why should I be in such trouble. And why should so many of us be in such trouble – I'm not an American for nothing, I'm socially minded, doc. Why are there so many of us in such trouble? Tell me doc. Give. And why should you, Dr Melville Cooper-Anstey, citizen of England, be sitting in that chair, in a position to dish out advice and comfort? Of course I know that you got all wrapped up in this thing because you, uh, kind of like people, doc, but after all, to kinda like people doc, puts you in a pretty privileged class for a start – so few citizens can afford to really kinda like people. So tell me doc, tell me . . .

Sergeant Musgrave's Dance *by John Arden*

John Arden was an important voice in British theatre between the late 1950s and the 1970s. This play is anti-imperialist and anti-war. In spite of the mixed reception to the first production at the Royal Court in 1959, it is considered a seminal work of the period.

The play is set in a poor, strike-ridden mining town in the north of England around the 1880s – the exact date is deliberately not given. It is 'realistic but not naturalistic', written in prose and verse and enriched with traditional folk tunes.

Three soldiers, led by Sergeant Musgrave, arrive in town on a cold winter's night, ostensibly on a recruiting drive. In fact they are deserters from a war in an overseas British protectorate where they have participated in a massacre to avenge a murdered comrade. The brutality of the event has overturned everything Musgrave believed in about the morality of war and the discipline of a soldier's life.

Musgrave is northern, working class and described by Arden as 'aged between thirty and forty, tall, swart, commanding, sardonic but never humorous'. He is not a clever man, but a hardened, seasoned soldier of eighteen years with an ingrained sense of discipline.

This is the recruitment scene in Act 3. A platform has been erected and the hungry miners have assembled in the market place to hear what Sergeant Musgrave has to say about joining up. This could be played as a straight recruitment speech (and it may suit you to play it in this way), but when you read the play you will see Musgrave has a very different agenda. Driven by a warped sense of logic, he is on a mission to kill twenty-five influential local dignitaries to avenge his comrade whom the people killed in the massacre. By doing this he hopes to awaken the townsfolk to the folly and brutality of war. This of course changes the agenda of the speech completely. It becomes angry, bitter and deeply ironic, increasing in urgency (as the stage directions indicate) as he describes the devastating effect of the Gatling gun. Attercliffe's short speech about how the gun works has been integrated here to help the flow.

When Musgrave is captured and waiting to be hanged, we are left with the conundrum of the pacifist message: why is the human instinct to respond to violence with yet more violence when it solves nothing?

———————————

Musgrave Now there's more tales than one about the Army, and a lot of funny jokers to run around and spread 'em, too. Aye, aye, we've all heard of 'em, we know all about 'em, and it's not my job this morning to swear to you what's true and what's not true. O' *course* you'll find there's an RSM here or a Provost-sarnt there what makes you cut the grass wi' nail-scissors, or dust the parade-ground with a toothbrush. It's all the bull, it's all in the game – but it's not what sends me here and it's not what put *these* on my arm, and it's nowt at all to do with *my* life, or these two with me, or any o' yours. So easy, me boys, don't think it. [(To the **Colliers**.) *There was another lad wi' you, in and out last night. He ought to be here.* (To the **Bargee**.) *Go and fetch him, will you? You know where he is.*

Bargee (finger to nose) *Ah. Ha ha. Aye aye.*

He slips out conspiratorially.

Musgrave (continues his speech) *I said, easy me boys, and don't think it.*] Because there's *work* in the Army, and bull's not right work, you can believe me on that – it's just foolery – any smart squaddy can carry it away like a tuppenny-ha'penny jam jar. So I'll tell you what the *work* is – open it up!

Attercliffe *flings open one of the boxes. It is packed with rifles. He takes one out and tosses it to* **Musgrave**.

Musgrave Now this is the rifle. This is what we term the butt of the rifle. This is the barrel. This here's the magazine. And this – (*he indicates the trigger*) – you should know what *this* is, you should know what it does . . . Well, the rifle's a good weapon, it's new, quick, accurate. This is the bayonet – (*he fixes his bayonet*) – it kills men smart, it's good and it's beautiful. But I've more to show than a rifle. Open it up!

Attercliffe *opens a second case. It contains a Gatling gun and tripod mounting.*

This is the newest, this is the smartest, call it the most beautiful. It's a Gatling gun, this. Watch how it works!

[*Attercliffe secures the gun to its mounting.*

Attercliffe] The rounds are fed to the chambers, which are arranged in a radial fashion, by means of a hopper-shaped aperture, *here*. Now pay attention while I go through the preliminary process of loading.

He goes through the preliminary process of loading.

[*Musgrave*] (*His urgency increasing all the time.*) The point being that here we've got a gun that doesn't shoot like: *Bang*, rattle-click-up-the-spout-what're-we-waiting-for, *bang*! But: Bang-bang-bang-bang-bang-bang-bang-bang-*bang* – and there's not a man alive in the whole of this marketplace. Modern times. Progress. Three hundred and fifty rounds in one minute – *flat!*

[The **Bargee** re-enters, soft-footed.

Musgrave (quickly to him) *Is he coming?*

The **Bargee** nods, finger to lips.

Attercliffe Now then, you see, the gun's loaded.

Musgrave] It didn't take long, you see.

[*Attercliffe No.*

Hirst gives a roll on the drums.

Attercliffe swivels the gun to face out into the audience.

Musgrave loads his rifle with a clip of cartridges.]

Musgrave (*His voice very taut and hard.*) The question remains as to the *use* of these weapons! (*He pushes his rifle-bolt home.*) You'll ask me: what's their purpose? Seeing we've beat the Russians in the Crimea, there's no war with France (there *may* be, but there isn't yet), and Germany's our friend, who do we have to fight? *Well*, the Reverend answered *that* for you, in his good short words. Me and my three lads – two lads, I'd say rather – we belong to a regiment is a few thousand miles from here, in a little country without much importance except from the point of view that there's a Union Jack flies over it and the people of that country can write British Subject after their names. And that makes us proud!

Poor Bitos *by Jean Anouilh*
(translated by Lucienne Hill)

This caustic black comedy was premiered at the Arts Theatre
in 1963. It is set in the halls of an old priory in a French
provincial town, ten years after the Second World War.

Maxime, a snobbish aristocrat has just inherited the
priory. He plans to sell it to Shell for conversion to a modern
garage as a snub to his docile ancestors who were tried and
guillotined there during the French Revolution. Before
signing it over, he hosts a fancy dress party to which his
guests are invited dressed as characters from the eighteenth
century. His chief reason for holding the party is to
humiliate Bitos, the town's hated Deputy Public Prosecutor,
who has been asked to come as Robespierre.

Bitos is a graceless, cruel, implacable, small-minded,
mean-spirited, rancorous little man. He comes from a
'second rate' background and exercises his office without
justice or mercy. He was known as 'beastly' Bitos at school,
a 'boring little scholarship boy who always came top.'
Maxime and his guests have loathed 'beastly' Bitos since
they were small boys, hating him for his working-class
origins and the cruel fanaticism with which he now
hounds and executes Nazi collaborators. They conspire to
humiliate him. Over supper they bait him mercilessly
under cover of their French Revolution personas. Incensed
by their attack, Bitos tries to leave – impotently threatening
legal sanctions – only to be met with the full force of
Maxime's hatred. It is to this that he responds in this
speech.

He reminds them of how he humiliated himself to be
their friend and how his mother's hard work paid for his
schooling. He presents himself as a victim who has risen
above their bourgeois snubs with diligence, self-sacrifice
and hard labour. His contempt for them and their kind is
clear; his sense of social inferiority almost visceral as he self-
righteously defends himself against their taunts.

Anouilh juggles past and present, reality and make-
believe, counterpointing Revolutionary France with French

provincial life in the 1950s – drawing parallels between Robespierrre's 'Reign of Terror' and that of Bitos, his modern counterpart.

Bitos (*after a very slight pause*) You're the only one whose dislike ever hurt me. Everybody always hated me at school because I always came first – and because I was a washer-woman's son! That's why they took me in for nothing. She washed your sheets, you little perverts – she washed your stained sheets for twenty years! It's those washed-out stains that have made me what I am – Doctor at Law and Philosophy, Bachelor of Science, History, Letters, Mathematics, German (*He yells, unaccountably.*) – and Italian! Funny, isn't it? I passed every examination it was possible to pass. When the others went off for a beer after lectures I went up to my room and sat alone over my books. And when they came back late at night, after their evenings out with girls, I was still at it. Until the markets opened; then I went to help unload the lorries. After that I slept three hours – when I had three left. And at the first lecture, there I was again, the first in my seat, in the front row, with my stupid great eyes open wide, to catch as much as I could of that precious bourgeois knowledge that my mother's soapy arms were paying for. (*He adds, calmer now, with a curious little gesture, venomous and yet prim.*) If ever I'm entitled to a family crest like you, gentlemen, it will have my mother's two red arms upon it – crossed.

Equus *by Peter Shaffer*

This is a disturbing play that deals with issues of parenting, religious fervour and perceptions of normality.

Martin Dysart is a child psychiatrist in his mid forties. Alan Strang, a seventeen-year-old boy, has been sent to him for treatment after being found guilty of blinding six horses with a metal spike. The play is a painful journey into Alan's mind and Dysart's own inner conflicts as he seeks ways to treat him.

Dysart's approach is to make Alan revisit the events that led to his crime. During treatment he finds out about Alan's background – his overly religious mother, his repressive and critical father, and the origins of Alan's obsessive relationship with horses, with its primitive sexual associations. We learn that Dysart has begun to question his profession and seriously doubt his value to the young people he treats.

This speech is the angry culmination of Dysart's self-doubt. He knows Alan has felt more passion than anything he has ever experienced. While he buries his head in academic books about mythology, Alan is 'taking the horse by the reins' and trying to become one outside his window. He equates what he does to his patients with Alan's crime – striking at his patient's heads and extinguishing that elemental spark. By 'curing' Alan and removing ecstasy at the core of his life, with what will he be leaving him?

Initially Dysart is responding to his colleague, Hester Salomon, the magistrate who originally referred Alan for psychiatric help. She asks Dysart to relieve Alan's pain, prompting him to turn on the audience with a storming, self-questioning rant. He equates 'normal' with 'tethered and 'tamed' If he consigns Alan to the fate of normality, what then? In a final desperate expression of a quest for the sublime, he acknowledges that it is the 'bit' of so called 'normality' that denies him the mysteries and miracles that Alan has shown him.

Dysart (*crying out*) *All right! I'll take it away!* He'll be delivered from madness. *What then?* He'll feel himself acceptable! *What then?* Do you think feelings like his can be simply re-attached, like plasters? Stuck on to other objects we select? *Look at him!* . . . My desire might be to make this boy an ardent husband – a caring citizen – a worshipper of abstract and unifying God. My achievement, however, is more likely to make a ghost! . . . Let me tell you exactly what I'm going to do to him!

He steps out of the square and walks round the upstage end of it, storming at the audience.

I'll heal the rash on his body. I'll erase the welts cut into his mind by flying manes. When that's done, I'll set him on a nice mini-scooter and send him puttering off into the Normal world where animals are treated *properly*: made extinct, or put into servitude, or tethered all their lives in dim light, just to feed it! I'll give him the good Normal world where we're tethered beside them – blinking our nights away in a non-stop drench of cathode-ray over our shrivelling heads! I'll take away his Field of Ha Ha, and give him Normal places for his ecstasy – multi-lane highways driven through the guts of cities, extinguishing Place altogether, *even the idea of Place!* He'll trot on his metal pony tamely through the concrete evening – and one thing I promise you: he will never touch hide again! With any luck his private parts will come to feel as plastic to him as the products of the factory to which he will almost certainly be sent. Who knows? He may even come to find sex funny. Smirky funny. Bit of grunt funny. Trampled and furtive and entirely in control. Hopefully, he'll feel nothing at his fork but Approved Flesh. *I doubt, however, with much passion!* . . . Passion, you see, can be destroyed by a doctor. It cannot be created.

He addresses **Alan** *directly, in farewell.*

You won't gallop any more, Alan. Horses will be quite safe. You'll save your pennies every week, till you can change that scooter in for a car, and put the odd 50p on the gee-gees, quite forgetting that they were ever anything more to you than bearers of little profits and little losses. You will, however, be without pain. More or less completely without pain.

Pause.

He speaks directly to the theatre, standing by the motionless body of **Alan Strang**, *under the blanket.*

And now for me it never stops: that voice of Equus out of the cave – 'Why Me? . . . Why Me? . . . Account for Me!' . . . All right – I surrender! I say it! . . . In an ultimate sense I cannot know what I do in this place – yet I do ultimate things. Essentially I cannot know what I do – yet I do essential things. Irreversible, terminal things. I stand in the dark with a pick in my hand, striking at heads.

He moves away from **Alan**, *back to the downstage bench, and finally sits.*

I need – more desperately than my children need me – a way of seeing in the dark. What way is this? . . . *What dark is this?* . . . I cannot call it ordained of God: I can't get that far. I will however pay it so much homage. There is now, in my mouth, this sharp chain. And it never comes out.

A long pause.

Dysart *sits staring.*

Confusions *by Alan Ayckbourn*

Confusions is a set of five short plays with interlinking themes of confusion, isolation, conflict and misunderstanding. It was written as a challenge to five actors who play all the parts and was first performed at the Apollo Theatre in 1976.

A Talk in the Park is the final play in the set and acts as something of a curtain call.

Five lonely characters come to the park for companionship and rehearse their preoccupations and obsessions to a neighbour on a bench. Like musical chairs, each character is driven to the next bench where they address their own obsessions before the listener moves on.

Arthur is 'a birdlike man in a long mackintosh, obviously on the lookout for company'. He approaches Beryl, a belligerent young girl engrossed in reading a letter, and immediately attempts to engage her in conversation. Beryl refuses to be drawn, but Arthur ploughs on regardless.

Arthur is an 'anorak'. He has no social skills. He is a sad, lonely little man, who is completely self-absorbed. Although of no particular age, he does not 'feel' young. His obsession with his collection of cigarette cards gives us some insight into the emptiness of his life. His view of himself as a 'collector of people' underlines his feelings of exclusion. He is a watcher rather than the participant he longs to be. His preference for the sweetness and wholesomeness of women seems to hark back to childhood and remembered warmth of his mother. What is Arthur's 'line of work'? One senses he is unemployed and rarely goes out except to the park. Poor Arthur's attempts to find company, to give himself some status in the world, underpin every line. His strategies for coping seem very fragile. He is subsumed by his need to make contact with other human beings. Unfortunately, in Beryl he has chosen someone with her own problems and she quickly moves on.

Arthur Mind you, I shouldn't be here. By rights, I should be at home. That's where I should be. Inside my front door. I've got plenty of things I should be doing. The kitchen shelves to name but three. Only you sit at home on a day like today. Sunday. Nothing to do. On your own – you think to yourself, this is no good, this won't get things done – and there you are talking to yourself. You know what they say about people who talk to themselves? Eh? Eh? Yes. So I thought it's outdoors for you, else they'll come and take you away. Mind you, I'm never at a loss. I'm a very fulfilled person. I have, for example, one of the biggest collections of cigarette cards of anyone alive or dead that I know of. And you don't get that by sitting on your behind all day. But I'll let you into a secret. Do you know what it is that's the most valuable thing there is you can hope to collect? People. I'm a collector of people. I look at them, I observe them, I hear them talk, I listen to their manner of speaking and I think, hallo, here's another one. Different. Different again. Because I'll let you into a secret. They are like fingerprints. They are never quite the same. And I've met a number in my lifetime. Quite a number. Some good, some bad, all different. But the best of them, and I'm saying this to you quite frankly and openly, the best of them are women. They are superior people. They are better people. They are cleaner people. They are kinder-hearted people. If I had a choice, I'd be a woman. Now that makes you laugh, I expect, but it's the truth. When I choose to have a conversation, I can tell you it's with a woman every time. Because a woman is one of nature's listeners. Most men I wouldn't give the time of day to. Now I expect that shocks you but it's the truth. Trouble is, I don't get to meet as many women as I'd like to. My particular line of work does not bring me into contact with them as much as I would wish. Which is a pity.

The Long and the Short and the Tall *by Willis Hall*

This play was first performed on the Edinburgh Fringe in 1958, transferred to the Royal Court the following year and was later made into a film. It is about war and the moral dilemmas faced by soldiers in wartime.

The action take place in a hut in the Malaysian jungle where a group of rookie soldiers have sought refuge during the Japanese advance on Singapore in 1942. They are under the command of Sergeant Mitchem, a seasoned combatant who understands the dangers and realities of war. He is fair and open minded but tough when he needs to be. He's a good commanding officer who cares about his men, knows that army discipline is the key to their safety and understands the value of staying calm in a crisis. The battery of the section's radio is flat and they have lost contact with base camp, so Mitchem has gone outside to study the lie of the land, leaving his Corporal, McLeish, in charge of the section. While he is away, tempers flare and regional rivalries are sparked between Scottish McLeish and cockney Private Bamforth. Sergeant Mitchem returns, just as the two are squaring up for a fight. Bamforth identifies himself as the chief culprit and Mitchem takes him brusquely and efficiently to task.

The speech breaks into two halves. In the first, Mitchem pulls rank. In archetypal 'army-speak' he gives Private Bamforth a dressing-down, publicly humiliating him and warning him of the direst consequences if he doesn't tow the line. In the second half, he lets the matter drop. The men are 'at ease' and the tone changes completely as he puts his men in the picture about the lie of the land and how they can safely make their way back to base.

Later in the play, a Japanese soldier stumbles into their hut and is taken prisoner. The men discover the Japanese army is marching towards them. All are tested to their limits when confronted with the 'enemy' and the harsh realities of 'action'.

Mitchem I've watched you, lad. I've had my eye on you. Ever since you first turned up. I've seen you try and come it on with every junior N.C.O. that's been made up. The barrack-room lawyer. The hard case. You can quote King's Regs from now until the middle of next week. Up to every dodge and skive that's in the book. There's just one thing. It doesn't work with me, 'cause I don't work according to the book. You don't know anything, Bamforth. You don't know anything at all. But if you want to try and come it on with me I'll tell you, here and now, that I can be a bastard. I can be the biggest bastard of them all. And just remember this: I've got three stripes start on you. You're a non-runner, son, I start favourite halfway down the course before the off. You haven't got a chance. So now just go ahead and play it how you want. I'm easy. (*Pause.*) Now get back into line the pair of you. Move! (**Macleish and Bamforth** *step back into the rank.* **Mitchem** *crosses to speak to* **Bamforth**.) And if you take my tip you'll stay in line. (**Mitchem** *steps back to address the patrol.*) Stand at ease! . . . Easy . . . (*The men relax.*) Now, pay attention – all of you. We've had a sortie round, Corporal Johnstone and myself; I'll try and put you in the picture now before we set off back. The main track is about sixty yards from here through the trees. The way we came – and that's the way we're going back. Round the back of here the undergrowth's so thick it would take a month of Sundays to hack half a mile. There's only one way out and that's where we came in. It's over fifteen miles from here to camp and we're moving off in fifteen minutes' time. We march at five-yard intervals – I don't want any of you closing up. Corporal Johnstone's breaking trail and I'll bring up the rear. There'll be no talking. I've said there'll be a five-yard interval between each man. You'll keep it that way. What goes for closing up goes twice as much for dropping back – I don't want any of you falling out. I've told you once it's fifteen miles, or thereabouts, to base. Due south. The other way – north – and twenty miles as near as we can estimate, the line's been built to keep the Nips at bay. All positions have been consolidated. Which means that all the mobs from round these parts have been moved up to the front – or most of them – a few have been withdrawn. There's not a living soul, apart from local wogs, if any, for miles from here. If any one of you gets lost he's on his own. I don't advise it. So you keep it five yards – dead. Anybody any questions?

Honour and Offer *by Henry Livings*

This play was first staged in Britain in 1969 after premiering in America the previous year. It is a comedy set in the orchard of Doris and Alfred Thring's pleasant cottage, around a couple of beehives.

Henry Cash is a discontented fifty-year-old bachelor who has lodged with the loving, if feckless Doris and Alfred for twelve years. He is a moneylender and secretary and treasurer of the Beekeepers Society. He is very much 'at home' with the Thrings, particularly so, as the deeds to their house are in his pocket as a result of Alfred's dodgy financial dealings. He is 'the very picture of probity,' rather dignified and yet, as he informs us in one of his frequent addresses to the audience, with 'a deep need to grasp his luscious landlady's haunches!' Alfred, a commercial traveller, is often overtaken by the need to grasp other people's haunches and tell a disgusted Henry all about it. To all outward appearances, Henry is a perfect gentleman, but inside he is a seething mass of lust, jealousy and self-righteousness.

This speech falls at the end of Act 1. Alfred has just got home from one of his trips and, after a spirited chase with Doris round the beehives, they have adjourned to the bedroom. Henry has been talking to Ernest, a fellow beekeeper about corruption in the local branch. The Thring's bedsprings clang joyously from the bedroom. Appalled by the dissolution of standards, Henry sees it as his duty to give a moral lead. His metaphor is the industry and business of bees.

Although Ernest has gone, Henry continues to speak to him as if he has not. This is something of a Biblical utterance. The first line of the speech is wonderfully onomatopoeic The repetition of Ernest's name implies a superior position in a world in which he sees himself as both teacher and philosopher, and not just on the question of bees! There is a warning for the idle and the lecherous. Praise for the decent and honest. No prizes for guessing who he means. Henry Livings clearly wants the actor to emphasise the words that are italicised. Doing so, along with relish in the language and long complex sentences, will give the speech the reflective pomposity it requires.

Henry The bees burble gently and go about their business in honest sincerity; it is an insult to their industry if we fail to trade in their production as diligently.

We neglect honey and pursue shallow self-interest at our peril.

Honour the little workers, Ernest, for with them lies our hopes of better things, they produce.

Nature provides, we must profit.

The latest and most scientific equipment . . . hives, trays, smoke-guns, veils and gloves etcetera, nationally approved and tested, as provided only by the secretary stroke treasurer; only the best is good enough. Trendy labels and modernistic jars, very good, yes. Yes, yes. Acceptable.

But decency and respect for the honey above all: nutritional, medicinal, extremely palatable, golden to the eye.

It is not proper that something so handsome and wholesome should be made the warrant for frivolity and peculation. The *bees* Ernest, guard the entrance to the hive with cold vigilance, woe to wasps.

The *bees* Ernest, decide their fate and act upon it in concert: when nectar and pollen are plentiful and the hive is too populous due to overproduction, the older workers *depart*, with their deposed queen, they *swarm*, note that: *They do not lie back in slothful ease.*

And the eggs laid by the queen are designated worker, drone or queen, according to need: the queen fertilizing the egg and the worker feeding the grub in those ways that will make it fulfil the role they require, note that: *each in his place under heaven.*

And the drones, Ernest, the *drones*, who live in functionless idleness until the queen requires to be fertilized, from amongst whom she chooses her consort, and tears his genitalia from him for her own; they shall be put out from the hive, pitilessly, when the best of them has mounted her and been spent. Note that: *the wages of idleness and lechery is death.*

The *bees,* Ernest have no legends, no myths, no history; they work, they build, they perpetuate themselves, each in his place and always, humbly identical to their forbears and their progeny; except, Ernest, for the brief but heroic stand of those fornicating drones; note it, Ernest.

A View from the Bridge *by Arthur Miller*

This play received its first London production at the Comedy Theatre in 1956. It borrows from the traditions of Greek tragedy, offering the audience a story to which they already know the outcome and asking them to consider the elemental forces that determine the life of the main character.

Eddie Carbone is a semi-literate Brooklyn longshoreman. He is a good family man who is well respected in Red Hook, a slum community of Italian and Sicilian immigrants. Eddie has brought up a young girl, Catherine, as his daughter and is deeply possessive of her. When she falls in love with an illegal Sicilian immigrant hiding in his house, he falls victim to feelings he can neither understand nor control. Rather than allow her to marry him, he denounces him to the Immigration Authorities, thereby losing his honour and respect in the community which cannot forgive his betrayal and which metes out its own primitive brand of justice.

This speech comes right at the beginning of the play after Eddie's fate has been sealed. It is addressed directly to the audience to introduce them to Eddie's story and social landscape.

Alfieri is a family lawyer who works in Red Hook and whose life has been dedicated to sorting out the trials and tribulations of his community. He is an Italian immigrant, 'in his fifties, tuning grey, portly, good-humoured and thought-ful,' who has lived in Brooklyn for a quarter of a century. When he says, 'justice is very important here', he means Sicilian rough justice rather than the US law he is paid to uphold. Red Hook is safer than it used to be, but he still remembers the bad old days of his compatriot Al Capone, when he had to keep a gun to hand. The psychology of Eddie and folks like him is well known to Alfieri who can trace their heritage back to the primitive ways of their homelands of Sicily and Calabria. He understands first-hand where this community's values are rooted.

Throughout the play Alfieri acts as a kind of 'Greek chorus', placing the action outside the confines of space and time. He is both inside and outside it – participating as

a plain speaking lawyer and at the same time commenting
on the inevitability of its course.

---

*Enter Alfieri, a lawyer in his fifties turning grey; he is portly, good-
humoured, and thoughtful. The two pitchers nod to him as he passes. He
crosses the stage to his desk, removes his hat, runs his fingers through his
hair, and grinning, speaks to the audience.*

Alfieri You wouldn't have known it, but something amusing has
just happened. You see how uneasily they nod to me? That's
because I am a lawyer. In this neighbourhood to meet a lawyer or a
priest on the street is unlucky. We're only thought of in connection
with disasters, and they'd rather not get too close.

I often think that behind that suspicious little nod of theirs lie three
thousand years of distrust. A lawyer means the law, and in Sicily,
from where their fathers came, the law has not been a friendly idea
since the Greeks were beaten.

I am inclined to notice the ruin in things, perhaps because I was
born in Italy. . . . I only came here when I was twenty-five. In those
days, Al Capone, the greatest Carthaginian of all, was learning his
trade on these pavements, and Frankie Yale himself was cut
precisely in half by a machine gun on the corner of Union Street,
two blocks away. Oh, there were many here who were justly shot by
unjust men. Justice is very important here.

But this is Red Hook, not Sicily. This is the slum that faces the bay
on the seaward side of Brooklyn Bridge. This is the gullet of New
York swallowing the tonnage of the world. And now we are quite
civilized, quite American. Now we settle for half, and I like it better.
I no longer keep a pistol in my filing cabinet.

And my practice is entirely unromantic.

My wife has warned me, so have my friends; they tell me the people
in this neighbourhood lack elegance, glamour. After all, who have I

dealt with in my life? Longshoremen and their wives, and fathers and grandfathers, compensation cases, evictions, family squabbles – the petty troubles of the poor – and yet . . . every few years there is still a case, and as the parties tell me what the trouble is, the flat air in my office suddenly washes in with the green scent of the sea, the dust in this air is blown away and the thought comes that in some Caesar's year, in Calabria perhaps or on the cliff at Syracuse, another lawyer, quite differently dressed, heard the same complaint and sat there as powerless as I, and watched it run its bloody course.

Eddie has appeared and has been pitching coins with the men and is highlighted among them. He is forty – a husky, slightly overweight longshoreman.

This one's name was Eddie Carbone, a longshoreman working the docks from Brooklyn Bridge to the breakwater where the open sea begins.

An Inspector Calls *by J. B. Priestley*

This play is set in the north Midlands in 1912. It is a critique of the middle classes as they move complacently towards the First World War. It received its first production in Moscow in 1945, was staged in London the following year, and found contemporary relevance in a recent high profile revival.

A small supper party is in full swing at the home of self-made industrialist Arthur Birling and wife Sybil. They are celebrating the engagement of their daughter Sheila to Gerald, the son of an aristocratic business rival. But when a man claiming to be a police inspector arrives to question them about the suicide of a young working-class girl, the hypocrisy at the heart of their middle-class respectability is exposed.

This speech comes near the beginning of the play. Gerald has just given Sheila her engagement ring. It seems an appropriate moment for Arthur to make a speech.

Priestley describes Birling as 'a heavy looking, rather portentous man in his middle fifties with fairly easy manners but rather provincial in his speech'. He is delighted with his daughter's engagement. He is a social climber and although business success has elevated him from his lower middle-class origins, Sheila's marriage promises to give him the business contacts and social status that have hitherto eluded him. He speaks as a 'hard-headed business man', a phrase he repeats three times! Arthur is the dominant male in his household who lives in a black and white world of lower costs and higher prices, where money is god and bigger and faster is better. He talks of the forthcoming marriage more as a convenient business arrangement than a love match. He is not an intellectual, nor does he have the grace of the class he aspires to. He is a stereotypical capitalist who despises the socialist values of the day, having made his money on the back of an exploited work force.

He is self-important, officious and vulgarly self-assertive, a bit of a 'barrack room lawyer' who refuses to be interrupted and who makes these strong, poorly supported, assertions – about the war, the Germans, Russia, the *Titanic* – without any substantiating knowledge.

It would be interesting to know what post-war audiences made of Arthur's arrogant predictions in the light of the world that they had recently inherited and the tragedy of the 'absolutely unsinkable' *Titanic*.

———————————

Birling (*rather heavily*) I just want to say this. (*Noticing that* **Sheila** *is still admiring her ring.*) Are you listening, Sheila? This concerns you too. And after all I don't often make speeches at you —

[**Sheila** *I'm sorry, Daddy. Actually I was listening.*]

She looks attentive, as they all do. He holds them for a moment before continuing.

I'm delighted about this engagement and I hope it won't be too long before you're married. And I want to say this. There's a good deal of silly talk about these days – *but* – and I speak as a hard-headed business man, who has to take risks and know what he's about – I say, you can ignore all this silly pessimistic talk. When you marry, you'll be marrying at a very good time. Yes, a very good time – and soon it'll be an even better time. Last month, just because the miners came out on strike, there's a lot of wild talk about possible labour trouble in the near future. Don't worry. We've passed the worst of it. We employers at last are coming together to see that our interests – and the interests of Capital – are properly protected. And we're in for a time of steadily increasing prosperity.

[**Gerald** *I believe you're right, sir.*

Eric *What abut war?*

Birling *Glad you mentioned it, Eric. I'm coming to that.*]

Just because the Kaiser makes a speech or two, or a few German officers have too much to drink and begin talking nonsense, you'll hear some people say that war's inevitable. And to that I say – fiddlesticks! The Germans don't want war. Nobody wants war, except some half-civilized folks in the Balkans. And why? There's

124

too much at stake these days. Everything to lose and nothing to gain by war.

[*Eric* *Yes, I know – but still –*]

Birling Just let me finish, Eric. You've a lot to learn yet. And I'm talking as a hard-headed, practical man of business. And I say there isn't a chance of war. The world's developing so fast that it'll make war impossible. Look at the progress we're making. In a year or two we'll have aeroplanes that will be able to go anywhere. And look at the way the automobile's making headway – bigger and faster all the time. And then ships. Why, a friend of mine went over this new liner last week – the *Titanic* – she sails next week – forty-six thousand eight hundred tons – forty-six thousand eight hundred tons – New York in five days – and every luxury – and unsinkable, absolutely unsinkable. That's what you've got to keep your eye on, facts like that, progress like that – and not a few German officers talking nonsense and a few scaremongers here making a fuss about nothing. Now you three young people, just listen to this – and remember what I'm telling you now. In twenty or thirty years' time – let's say, in 1940 – you may be giving a little party like this – your son or daughter might be getting engaged – and I tell you, by that time you'll be living in a world that'll have forgotten all these Capital versus Labour agitations and all these silly little war scares. There'll be peace and prosperity and rapid progress everywhere – except of course in Russia, which will always be behindhand naturally.

[*Mrs Birling* *Arthur!*]

As **Mrs Birling** *shows signs of interrupting.*

Birling Yes, my dear, I know – I'm talking too much. But you youngsters just remember what I said. We can't let these Bernard Shaws and H. G. Wellses do all the talking. We hard-headed practical business men must say something sometime. And we don't guess – we've had experience – and we *know*.

The Insect Play *by Karel Čapek*
(translated by Peter Majer and Cathy Porter)

This is an expressionistic, anti-war satire in which actors play a range of insects, from scavenging dung beetles to libidinous butterflies. Its structure is a series of playlets portraying a world in which insects' behaviour mirrors the worst attributes of humankind. The play was premiered in Prague in 1922. Čapek was an influential artist in post-war Europe and this is his most performed play.

This is the Prologue to the play. It introduces us to the garrulous Traveller, who is both the play's narrator and a watchful participant in the action, immediately establishing the play's energetic theatrical style and the Traveller's relationship with the audience. The speech is addressed straight into the audience's eye and performed with the exaggerated self-dramatising gesture typical of someone who 'has had a few over the eight!'

The Traveller is certainly drunk, despite his denials, falling flat on his face as he makes his first entrance. The fall is of course designed to get a laugh and the Traveller immediately responds to it by haranguing the audience from the ground. He expects no less than mockery. Life has dealt him some poor cards and his outlook is pessimistic. Notice he is given no name except that which other people call him – 'man'. It emphasises not only his lowly position in the world, but also his function in the play. Unlike the flower he addresses and envies, he is rootless – a vagrant and refugee from war in his own country. As a displaced outsider, he has been pushed from pillar to post by his fellow man, learning from bitter experience to despise them.

Traveller (*stumbles on from the wings, trips and falls, shouts at the audience*) Go on, laugh! Funny, isn't it? What the fuck. I'm not hurt. See how I fell? Straight as an arrow! Like a hero! I was . . . representing the Fall of Man! (*Lies on the ground, leaning on his elbow.*) Think I'm drunk? No way. Everything else is spinning. Round and round . . . (*Turns his head as though on a merry-go-round, then laughs maniacally.*) Stop, let me off, I'm going to be sick! (*Looks around.*) See what I mean? Everything's spinning. The whole planet. The whole universe. Just for me. What an honour. (*Straightens his clothes.*) Sorry, I'm not dressed to be the centre of all this cosmic harmony. (*Throws his cap on the ground.*) There, that's your centre now. Spin round her, she's strong . . . So I took a tumble, under my cross. You thought I was pissed too, little flower? Don't be so stuck-up, just because you're sober. Camomile, good for cuts – here's my heart, mend that. If I had roots like you, I wouldn't be wandering from place to place, would I? (*Belches.*) And if I didn't wander, I wouldn't know everything I know. Seen it all, I have. I was in the big war, learned some Latin, put my hand to anything – shovelling shit, sweeping the street. Everything no one else would touch, that's me. They know me everywhere. Man, they call me. You're under arrest, man. Move your arse, man. Sod off, man. Doesn't bother me if they call me man. Mind you, if I say give us a quid, man, they run a mile! (*Addressing a member of the audience.*) You got a problem, man? I'll call you what I like, right? Butterfly, dung-beetle, ant. Man or insect, I'm not bothered. I don't make trouble. Can't help seeing things, though. If I had roots in the earth I'd stare up at the sky (*Raises himself up on his knees.*), the very heavens above! Lovely! I could spend my whole life looking up there! (*Stands up, pointing at another member of the audience.*) But I can't, can I – I'm man! I have to look at my fellow-men. What a sight!

Sleuth *by Anthony Shaffer*

This is a witty and suspenseful parody of an Agatha Christie-style country house thriller. It explores the issue of sexual jealousy between a younger and older man. First performed in 1970, it was subsequently made into a film starring Sir Lawrence Olivier and Michael Caine. Good territory for your research!

Andrew Wyke is a rich, snobbish, self-congratulatory, 'old-school' author of detective fiction who lives in a grand sixteenth-century manor house in Wiltshire. He is described in the stage directions as a 'strongly built, tall fleshy man of fifty-seven, gone slightly to seed. His fair hair carries on it the suspicion that chemical aid has been invoked to keep the grey at bay.'

He invites a lower-class, younger and far less well-healed acquaintance, Milo Tindle, round to his house for a chat. His opening gambit, 'So you want to marry my wife,' reveals the real reason for the invitation! Professing himself glad to be rid of an expensive encumbrance, he engages Milo in a foolproof plan to steal his wife's jewellery and claim on the insurance. The plan, however, is not what it seems. It is the first step in a deadly game of revenge.

At this point Milo has been persuaded to disguise himself as a burglar to fake the robbery. Andrew has a gun and makes it clear to the out-manoeuvred Milo that he is going to kill him. In this speech he is cold-bloodedly playing with the dramatic possibilities of Milo's imminent demise. The most effective position for the body should be found. The method of dispatch. The casual, graphically enacted conversation with a police inspector after the event. He plays with the ideas in cool, abstract and practised tones, aping the language of his own detective fiction and toying with the terrified Milo with casual malevolence. It is almost as if he is considering the plot options for his next book. After rejecting a gory option, described with melodramatic relish, his tone becomes menacing and full of murderous intent as he forces his snivelling rival to mount the stairs to a real execution.

Andrew is smug and conceited enough to think he can

get away with the perfect murder, but the plot will reveal a determined and inventive opponent.

Andrew You should be flattered by the honour I'm doing you – to take your life lightheartedly – to make your death the centre piece of an arranged bit of fun. To put it another way, your demise will recreate a noble mind.

[*Milo This is where I came in.*

Andrew And where you go out, I'm afraid.] The only question to be decided is where the police shall find you. Sprawled over the desk like countless colonels in countless studies? Or propped up in the log basket like a rag doll? Which do you think? Early Agatha Christie or middle Nicholas Blake?

[*Milo For Christ's sake, Andrew, this is not a detective story, this is real life. You are talking of doing a real murder. Or killing a real man – don't you understand?*

Andrew Perhaps I shouldn't do it with a gun at all. Perhaps I should shove the ham knife into you, and leave you face down in the iddle of the room (melodramatic voice) – *your blood staining the flagstones a deep carmine.*]

Milo shudders.

[*Milo Oh God!*]

Andrew Or best of all, how about a real 1930's murder weapon – the mashie niblick. I've got one in my golf bag.

Andrew *fetches the golf club from the hall.* **Milo** *dives for the telephone but is too late.*

You would be discovered in the fireplace, I think in a fair old mess. (*Dramatic voice.*) The body lay on its back, its limbs grotesquely splayed like a broken puppet. The whole head had been pulped as if by some superhuman force. (**Inspector's voice.**) 'My God,' breathed the Inspector, blenching. 'Thompson, you'd better get a tarpaulin . . . Excuse me, sir, but was all this violence strictly necessary?' (*Own voice.*) I'm sorry Inspector. It was when I saw him handling my wife's nightdresses. I must have completely lost control of myself. (**Inspector**'s *voice.*) 'That's quite alright sir. Don't get excited. I quite understand.' (**Andrew** *throws down golf club.*) No. I don't like it. I think the scene the police find is simply this. After the fight you flee up the stairs to regain your ladder. I catch you on the landing and in the renewed struggle I shoot you. Nothing succeeds like simplicity, don't you agree, Milo? Now then, some of my own finger prints on my own revolver. (**Andrew** *takes his glove off and holds the gun in his naked hand.*) On your feet, up!

Andrew *forces* **Milo** *to mount the stairs by shoving the gun in his back.* **Milo** *gives a sudden spasmodic shudder.*

Did you know that Charles I put on two shirts the morning of his execution? 'If I tremble with cold,' he said, 'my enemies will say it was from fear; I will not expose myself to such reproaches.' You must also attempt dignity as you mount the steps to the scaffold.

Waiting for Godot *by Samuel Beckett*

Since its first performance in Paris in 1952, *Waiting for Godot* has been considered a classic of twentieth-century literature. Its plot is deceptively simple, taking place over two days in two Acts. It has been described as 'the play in which nothing happens twice!'

Two vaudeville tramps, Estragon and Vladimir, wait by a bare, black tree on a country road for the arrival of Godot. At the end of each Act a boy comes to tell them that Mr Godot cannot come today but will come tomorrow, and so the waiting goes on. In a struggle to pass time they argue, question and insult each other, reminisce, eat and contemplate hanging themselves from the tree. They are interrupted by two other characters: Pozzo and his hapless slave Lucky who is attached to his master by a rope, driven by a whip, and forced to carry Pozzo's many items of luggage, which he rarely puts down. He can only think and speak when wearing his hat and ordered to do so by his master.

Here he has been commanded by Pozzo to 'think' in order to entertain Estragon and Vladimir. In response he bursts into this chaotic performance of thinking aloud which comes out in an unpunctuated, seemingly meaningless babble with crazy juxtapositions and no grammatical structure or logical thought processes. Note the stage directions: 'Lucky . . . shouts his text'. Language appears to have completely broken down as a tool of communication. Is it the meaning of what Lucky says that is important, or is it the impulse that drives him to say it?

The language is littered with vulgar humour, puns and references to theology, philosophy and science. You feel there must be a logical argument buried somewhere in there, but it eludes you. Is it a diatribe about the indifference of heaven? The transience of man? It sounds like academic discourse, but nothing makes sense. To Lucky, though, it makes perfect sense, just as the speech of a drunk or a madman does to the speaker. The actor's job is to make the irrational sound rational; the illogical seem logical. This is the longest speech in the play, a tour de force that builds in agitation and animation until Lucky is finally set upon by the others and silenced by the removal of his hat.

Who is Godot? What do these surreal displaced characters represent? Despite a host of interpretations, Beckett maintained *Waiting for Godot* had no symbolic significance. Once, when asked in an interview what the play meant, he replied 'If I knew, I would have put it in the play'! What do you think?

Lucky Given the existence as uttered forth in the public works of Puncher and Wattmann of a personal God quaquaquaqua with white beard quaquaquaqua outside time without extension who from the heights of divine apathia divine athambia divine aphasia loves us dearly with some exceptions for reasons unknown but time will tell and suffers like the divine Miranda with those who for reasons unknown but time will tell are plunged in torment plunged in fire whose fire flames if that continues and who can doubt it will fire the firmament that is to say blast hell to heaven so blue still and calm so calm with a calm which even though intermittent is better than nothing but not so fast and considering what is more that as a result of the labours left unfinished crowned by the Acacacacademy of Anthropopopometry of Essy-in-Possy of Testew and Cunard it is established beyond all doubt all other doubt than that which clings to the labours of men that as a result of the labours unfinished of Testew and Cunard it is established as hereinafter but not so fast for reasons unknown that as a result of the public works of Puncher and Wattmann it is established beyond all doubt that in view of the labours of Fartov and Belcher left unfinished for reasons unknown of Testew and Cunard left unfinished it is established what many deny that man in Possy of Testew and Cunard that man in Essy that man in short that man in brief in spite of the strides of alimentation and defecation is seen to waste and pine waste and pine and concurrently simultaneously what is more for reasons unknown in spite of the strides of physical culture the practice of sports such as tennis football running cycling swimming flying floating riding

gliding conating camogie skating tennis of all kinds dying flying
sports of all sorts autumn summer winter winter tennis of all kinds
hockey of all sorts penicilline and succedanea in a word I resume
and concurrently simultaneously for reasons unknown to shrink
and dwindle in spite of the tennis I resume flying gliding golf over
nine and eighteen holes tennis of all sorts in a word for reasons
unknown in Feckham Peckham Fulham Clapham namely
concurrently simultaneously what is more for reasons unknown but
time will tell to shrink and dwindle I resume Fulham Clapham in a
word the dead loss per caput since the death of Bishop Berkeley
being to the tune of one inch four ounce per caput approximately
by and large more or less to the nearest decimal good measure
round figures stark naked in the stockinged feet in Connemara in a
word for reasons unknown no matter what matter the facts are there
and considering what is more much more grave that in the light of
the labours lost of Steinweg and Peterman it appears what is much
more grave that in the light the light the light of the labours lost of
Steinweg and Peterman that in the plains in the mountains by the
seas by the rivers running water running fire the air is the same and
then the earth namely the air and then the earth in the great cold
the great dark the air and the earth abode of stones in the great cold
alas alas in the year of their Lord six hundred and something the air
the earth the sea the earth abode of stones in the great deeps the
great cold on sea on land and in the air I resume for reasons
unknown in spite of the tennis the facts are there but time will tell I
resume alas alas on on in short in fine on on abode of stones who
can doubt it I resume but not so fast I resume the skull to shrink
and waste and concurrently simultaneously what is more for
reasons unknown in spite of the tennis on on the beard the flames
the tears the stones so blue so calm alas alas on on the skull the
skull the skull the skull in Connemara in spite of the tennis the
labours abandoned left unfinished graver still abode of stones in a
word I resume alas alas abandoned unfinished the skull the skull in
Connemara in spite of the tennis the skull alas the stones Cunard
(*Mêlee, final vociferations.*) tennis . . . the stones . . . so calm . . .
Cunard . . . unfinished . . .

Ubu Rex *by Alfred Jarry (translated by Cyril Connolly and Simon Watson Taylor)*

Alfred Jarry is best known for his three Ubu plays which started out as puppet shows and were devised with teenage friends to lampoon their physics teacher. They are seen as theatre's first pieces of absurdist drama and have had a profound influence on both the French surrealist movement and the work of Beckett and Ionesco.

The first play, *Ubu Rex,* was premiered in France in 1896. It mirrors Shakespeare's *Macbeth* and can be seen as a sideswipe at society's empty values and the indifference and cruelty of our masters. Ubu's first word, 'Merdre' not 'Merde' – translated as 'Pschitt' rather than 'Shit' – sets the play's anarchic tone and the keynote for Jarry's idiosyncratic language. It was received with a mixture of outrage and controversy by the chattering classes of the day.

Pa Ubu is a repellent old man who, with his equally awful wife, Ma Ubu, usurps the throne of Poland by every foul means. He is a grotesque, oafish, murderous, idiotic dictator – a larger than life character who is self-interested, cruel, manipulative and over-indulgent. He embodies everything that is rotten and stupid in the human race. Once he achieves power he embarks on a brutal and tyrannical rule until he is driven from the land by opposing forces.

This scene comes towards the end of the play. The Ubus have been dethroned after a terrific battle and forced to flee. Ma Ubu has deserted her husband and run off with the state treasure. Pa Ubu escapes the battle, and an altercation with a bear, and hides in a copse with his exhausted and hungry henchmen. Here, he is talking in his sleep. He relives recent danger and pursuit and harangues his treacherous wife and the opposing forces led by Captain Macnure (M'Nure), who he here confuses with the bear. He sees himself dead and buried with other 'great men' of Poland, and revels in the horrid retributions his 'phynance extortioners' visit on the enemy. In this speech we are overhearing the garbled articulation of his dream in a shifting landscape of time and space. It is a kaleidoscope of fearful imaginings, bravado, self-aggrandisement, wish fulfilment and spleen.

This play pays no lip service to social realism. Jarry's characters are vulgar, shockingly dehumanised, and over the top. The language is gross, colourful and often invented – as in 'phynance' – or slightly twisted – as in 'nearoles'. The style is energetic and broad brush. Think Punch and Judy; think vaudeville; think pantomime; think *Monty Python*; think *The Goons,* and you will begin to have some understanding of Jarry's surreal and exuberant world.

––––––––––––––––––

Pa Ubu (*talking in his sleep*) Hey, mister Russian dragoon, Sir, don't shoot in this direction, there's someone here. Ah! there's M'Nure, he's got a nasty look about him, just like a bear. And there's Boggerlas coming after me! The bear, the bear! Ah, it's down! What a tough monster, great God! No, I won't lend a hand. Go away, Boggerlas! Do you hear me, you lout? Here's Renski now, and the Tsar! Oh! they're going to hit me. Ugh, there's madam my female! Where did you get all that gold? You've stolen my gold, you slut, you've been scrabbling around in my tomb which is in Warsaw Cathedral, not far from the Moon. I've been dead a long time, yes, it's Boggerlas who killed me and I'm buried at Warsaw by the side of Ladislas the Great, and also at Cracow by the side of Jan Sigismund, and also at Thorn in the casemate with M'Nure! There it is again. Be off with you, accursed bear. You look just like M'Nure. And you smell just like M'Nure. Do you hear me, beast of Satan? No, he can't hear me, the Phynance-extortioners have perforated his nearoles. Debraining, killing off, perforation of nearoles, money grabbing and drinking oneself to death, that's the life for a Phynance-extortioner, and the Master of Phynances revels in such joys.

He falls silent and sleeps.

Noah *by André Obey*
(translated by Arthur Wilmurt)

Obey wrote *Noah* between 1929 and 1930. He used the story of the Flood as its inspiration and medieval mystery and miracle plays as the model for the idiom. Its theme of global catastrophe and hopeful renewal seem prescient of the Second World War, but Obey disclaimed any such intention.

Noah is a simple, warm-hearted farmer with a homely wife and five teenage children.

This is the first speech of the play. The language is direct, modern and colloquial. No lip service is paid to its biblical context. Noah has all but finished constructing the Ark. He is happy in his work and sings as he double-checks his measurements. He's pretty pleased with himself. For a farmer he has become quite a good carpenter in the last year.

Initially, Noah tries to attract the Busy Man's attention. He wants advice on how to proceed. He needs a decision about whether he should make a rudder! On hearing there is not to be one, his attitude changes. His exchanges with God are a bit like hearing one half of a telephone conversation from which you can deduce the responses at the other end. God is running out of patience with Noah's stupid questions, while Noah treats God like an irascible friend who can be forgiven because he has rather a lot on his mind. God should be as tangible a presence on stage as Noah.

The speech has an interesting dynamic. Noah seems almost to be 'playing to the gallery'. Aware the audience is eavesdropping on his conversation with God, he demonstrates the closeness of his relationship through the chatty intimacy of his speech. Look how he starts to spell out 'rudder' to get his point across. His boisterous imitations of wind and storm are not only for the audience's benefit but to diffuse a frightening prospect for himself as well. 'Storms? I can handle storms. *No* problem', is the subtext here. The repetition of 'I'm ready' betrays his worries about setting out in a rudderless boat. He trusts the Almighty to look after him in a crisis, but bangs a few more nails in just in case!

In the final analysis Noah is content to obey the commandments of God in whom he has placed his trust – even though His grand purpose escapes him. Once The Ark is finished, the oppressive heat presages the coming storm and a watchful Noah is on tenterhooks as to how and when it will all begin.

———————

A glade. The Ark is at the right, only the poop deck showing, with a ladder to the ground. **Noah** *is taking measurements and singing a little song. He scratches his head and goes over the measurements again. Then he calls:*

Noah (*softly*) Lord . . . (*Louder.*) Lord . . . (*Very loud.*) Lord! . . . Yes, Lord, it's me. Extremely sorry to bother You again, but . . . What's that? Yes, I know You've other things to think of, but after I've once shoved off, won't it be a little late? . . . Oh, no, Lord, no, no, no . . . No, Lord, please don't think that. . . . Oh, but naturally, of course, I trust You! You could tell me to set sail on a plank – a branch – on just a cabbage leaf. . . . Yes, You could even tell me to put out to sea with nothing but my loincloth, even without my loincloth – completely — (*He has gone down on his knees, but he gets up immediately.*) Yes, yes, Lord, I beg Your pardon. I know Your time is precious. Well, this is all I wanted to ask You: Should I make a rudder? I say, a rudder. . . . No, no, Lord. R for Robert; U for Una; D for . . . that's it, a rudder. Good . . . very good, I never thought of that. Of course, winds, currents, tides . . . What was that, Lord? Storms? Oh, and while You're there just one other little thing. . . . Are You listening, Lord? (*To the audience.*) Gone!! . . . He's in a bad temper. . . . Well, you can't blame Him; He has so much to think of. All right; no rudder. (*He considers the ark.*) Tides, currents, winds. (*He imitates the winds.*) Psch! . . . Psch! . . . Storms. (*He imitates the tempests.*) Vloum! Be da Bloum! Oh, that's going to be (*he makes a quick movement*) simply . . . magnificent!! . . . No, no, Lord I'm not afraid. I know that You'll be with me. I was only trying to imagine . . . Oh, Lord, while You're there I'd like just to ask . . . (*To the* *audience.*) Che! Gone again. You see how careful you have to be. (*He laughs.*) He was listening all the time. (*He goes to the Ark.*) Storms! . . . I think I'll just put a few more nails in down here. (*He hammers and sings.*)

When the boat goes well, all goes well.

When all goes well, the boat goes well.

(*He admires his work.*) And when I think that a year ago I couldn't hammer a nail without hitting my thumb. That's pretty good, if I do say so myself. (*He climbs aboard the Ark and stands there like a captain.*) Larboard and starboard! . . . Cast off the hawsers! . . . Close the portholes! . . . 'Ware shoals! . . . Wait till the squall's over! . . . Now I'm ready, completely ready, absolutely ready! I'm ready. (*He cries to Heaven.*) I am ready! (*Then quietly.*) Well, I should like to know how all this business is going to begin. (*He looks all around, at the trees, the bushes, and the sky.*) Magnificent weather – oppressively hot and no sign of a cloud. Well, that part of the programme is His look-out.

Acknowledgements

p.102   extract from *Poor Bitos* by Jean Anouilh, from *Anouilh Plays 1*, Methuen Publishing Ltd. Copyright © 1964 Jean Anouilh & Lucienne Hill. Performance rights: Alan Brodie Representation Ltd, 211 Piccadilly, London, W1J 9HF, www.alanbrodie.com.

p.98   extract from *Serjeant Musgrave's Dance* by John Arden, from *Arden Plays 1*, Methuen Publishing Ltd. Copyright © 1960 by John Arden. Performance rights: Casarotto Ramsay & Associates Ltd, 60-66 Wardour Street, London, W1V 4ND, www.casarotto.uk.com.

p.108   extract from *Confusions* by Alan Ayckbourn, Methuen Publishing Ltd. Copyright © 1977 by Redburn Productions Ltd. Professional performance rights: Casarotto Ramsay & Associates Ltd, London, W1V 4ND, www.casarotto.uk.com. Amateur performance rights: Samuel French Ltd, 52 Fitzroy Street, London, W1T 5JR, www.samuelfrench-london.co.uk.

p.133   extract from *Waiting for Godot* by Samuel Beckett, Faber & Faber Ltd. Estate representative: Curtis Brown Group Ltd, Haymarket House, 28-29 Haymarket, London, SW1Y 4SP. Amateur performance rights: Samuel French Ltd, 52 Fitzroy Street, London, W1T 5JR, www.samuelfrench-london.co.uk.

p.93   extract from *The Quare Fellow* by Brendan Behan, from *Behan Complete Plays*, Methuen Publishing Ltd. Copyright © 1956 by Brendan Behan and Theatre Workshop. Professional performance rights: The Sayle Literary Agency, Bickerton House, 25-27 Bickerton Road, London, N19 5JT. Amateur performance rights: Samuel French Ltd, 52 Fitzroy Street, London, W1T 5JR, www.samuelfrench-london.co..uk.

p.86   extract from *A Man for All Seasons* by Robert Bolt, Methuen

p.27   extract from *The White Liars* by Peter Shaffer, Penguin
       Books. Copyright © Peter Shaffer. Performance rights: MLR
       Ltd, 200 Fulham Road, London, SW10 9PN.

p.18   extract from *The Music Cure* by George Bernard Shaw.
       Copyright © The Estate of George Bernard Shaw.
       Performance rights: The Society of Authors, 84 Drayton
       Gardens, London, SW10 9SB, www.thesocietyofauthors.org.

p.12   extract from *Rosencrantz and Guildenstern are Dead* by Tom
       Stoppard, Faber & Faber Ltd. Copyright © 1967 Tom
       Stoppard. Professional performance rights: PFD, 34-43
       Russell Street, London, WC2B 5HA, www.pfd.co.uk.
       Amateur performance rights: Samuel French Ltd, 52 Fitzroy
       Street, London, W1T 5JR, www.samuelfrench-london.co.uk.

p.84   extract from *Travesties* by Tom Stoppard, Faber & Faber Ltd.
       Copyright © 1975 Tom Stoppard. Professional performance
       rights: PFD, 34-43 Russell Street, London, WC2B 5HA,
       www.pfd.co.uk. Amateur performance rights: Samuel
       French Ltd, 52 Fitzroy Street, London, W1T 5JR,
       www.samuelfrench-london.co.uk.

p.22   extract from *The Playboy of the Western World* by J M Synge
       from *Synge Complete Plays* (Methuen Publishing Ltd).

p.7   extract from *Spring Awakening* by Frank Wedekind,
       Methuen Publishing Ltd. Translation copyright © 1980,
       1993 by Edward Bond & Elisabeth Bond-Pablé. Performance
       rights: Casarotto Ramsay & Associates Ltd, 60-66 Wardour
       Street, London, W1V 4ND, www.casarotto.uk.com.

p.31   extract from *The Kitchen* by Arnold Wesker. Published by
       Jonathan Cape and used by kind permission of The
       Random House Group Ltd. Performance rights: David
       Higham Associates Ltd, 5-8 Lower John Street, Golden
       Square, London, W1F 9HA.

p.59   extract from *The Devils* by John Whiting. Originally published by Heinemann in 1961. Copyright © The Estate of John Whiting. Professional performance rights: PFD, 34-43 Russell Street, London, WC2B 5HA, www.pfd.co.uk. Amateur performance rights: Samuel French Ltd, 52 Fitzroy Street, London, W1T 5JR, www.samuelfrench-london.co.uk.

p.39   extract from *The Glass Menagerie* by Tennessee Williams, Methuen Publishing Ltd. Copyright © 1945, renewed 1973 The University of the South, USA. Professional performance rights: Georges Borchardt, Inc., 136 East 57th Street, New York, NY 10022, USA. Amateur performance rights: Samuel French Ltd, 52 Fitzroy Street, London, W1T 5JR, www.samuelfrench-london.co.uk. US & Canadian performance rights: The Dramatists Play Service, Inc., 440 Park Avenue South, New York, NY 10016, USA, www.dramatists.com.

Disclaimer